DK EYEWITNESS

T0063859

TOP**10**
HONG KONG

Top 10 Hong Kong Highlights

The Top 10 of Everything

CONTENTS

Hong Kong Area by Area

Streetsmart

Within each Top 10 list in this book, no hierarchy of quality or popularity is implied. All 10 are, in the editor's opinion, of roughly equal merit.

Title page, front cover and spine *The stunning skyline of Hong Kong, as seen from the Peak* ***Back cover, clockwise from top left*** *Junk boat in Victoria Harbour; IFC shopping mall; busy Kowloon street; Hong Kong skyline; Big Buddha and Po Lin Monastery*

The rapid rate at which the world is changing is constantly keeping the DK Eyewitness team on our toes. While we've worked hard to ensure that this edition of Hong Kong is accurate and up-to-date, we know that opening hours alter, standards shift, prices fluctuate, places close and new ones pop up in their stead. So, if you notice we've got something wrong or left something out, we want to hear about it. Please get in touch at travelguides@dk.com

Welcome to
Hong Kong

A quiet island of fishing villages that transformed into a hub of international trade, Hong Kong has a rich heritage and unique culture. The ancient temples, bustling markets, tall skyscrapers, beautiful beaches and imposing mountains combine to make it one of Asia's most exciting territories. With DK Eyewitness Top 10 Hong Kong, it's yours to explore.

We love Hong Kong: the buzzing atmosphere, the futuristic harbourside cityscapes, the forward-looking mentality. What could be better than shopping for designer fashion in **Tsim Sha Tsui**'s malls, looking down over the frenetic city from the cool heights of **The Peak**, riding the romantic **Star Ferry** between Kowloon and Hong Kong Island or joining the revelers for a night at the **Happy Valley Racecourse**. It's all here, packed into this tiny territory on China's Pearl River Delta.

Yet Hong Kong isn't all just glitz and glamour. Along with the cities of **Macau**, **Shenzhen** and **Guangzhou**, there are centuries of history here. Embrace a city of myriad cultures inside smoky temples, at dawn tai chi sessions in the parks, in traditional **New Territory** villages, or among the bustling market stalls. The packed calendar of events tops off this exciting city, from the annual **Rugby Sevens** to the captivating firework displays that ring in the **Chinese New Year**.

Whether you're visiting for a weekend or a week, our Top 10 guide brings together the best of everything the region has to offer, from **Tai Long Wan**'s best beaches to the hottest nightclubs in **Lan Kwai Fong**. The guide has useful tips throughout, from seeking out what's free to places off the beaten track, plus 11 easy-to-follow itineraries, designed to tie together a clutch of sights in a short space of time. Add inspiring photography and detailed maps, and you have the essential pocket-sized travel companion. **Enjoy the book, and enjoy Hong Kong**.

Clockwise from top: Junk boat in Victoria Harbour, tai chi practice, Clock Tower in Kowloon, Lan Kwai Fong, Ten Thousand Buddhas Monastery, Peak Tower, Po Lin Monastery

Exploring Hong Kong

For the sheer variety of things to see and do, visitors to Hong Kong are spoiled for choice. Whether you are here for a short stay or just wanting a flavour of this great city, you need to make the most of your time. From jaw-dropping cityscape views to remote tropical beaches, here are some ideas for two and four days of sightseeing in Hong Kong.

The Peak Tram provides its passengers with some of the best views of Central's skyscrapers as it climbs to the top.

Man Mo Temple is dedicated to the gods of war and literature.

Two Days in Hong Kong

Day ❶
MORNING
Begin on Hong Kong Island with a tasty dim sum breakfast, then follow **Hollywood Road** *(see p67)* to **Man Mo Temple** *(see p67)*. Continue to **Central's Statue Square** *(see pp14–15)* to admire the modern architecture.
AFTERNOON
Head to **Stanley** *(see pp20–21)* for low-key beaches and dinner. Ascend **The Peak** *(see pp12–13)* for city views during the show, A Symphony of Lights (8pm daily), before downing a nightcap at **Lan Kwai Fong** *(see p66)*.

Day ❷
MORNING
Catch an early ferry to Lantau Island and ride on the Ngong Ping 360 cable car to the **Big Buddha and Po Lin Monastery** *(see pp32–3)*.
AFTERNOON
Head to **Kowloon Park** *(see p87)* to people-watch, or on Sundays to see a martial art display at its Kung Fu Corner (2:30–4:30pm). After shopping along **Nathan Road** *(see p43)*, wander **Temple Street Night Market** *(see pp22–3)* for picking up a souvenir and some alfresco dining at a *dai pai dong*. Round off the evening with a cocktail at **Felix Restaurant** *(see p50)*.

Four Days in Hong Kong

Day ❶
MORNING
Ascend **The Peak** *(see pp12–13)* for glorious views over the city and its islands, and glimpse some of the world's most expensive properties.

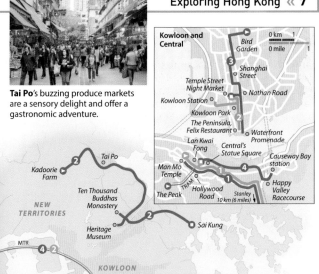

Tai Po's buzzing produce markets are a sensory delight and offer a gastronomic adventure.

AFTERNOON
Check out **Hollywood Road** *(see p67)* and **Man Mo Temple** *(see p67)* before heading to **Stanley** *(see pp20–21)*. End the day with an evening meal here or at beachside **Shek O** village *(see p81)*.

Day ❷
MORNING
Spend the whole morning at **Kadoorie Farm** *(see p108)*.
AFTERNOON
After lunch from the markets at **Tai Po** *(see p112)* spend a while at the **Heritage Museum** *(see pp26–7)* and **Ten Thousand Buddhas Monastery** *(see p107)*, before heading to **Sai Kung** *(see p110)* for a seafood meal.

Day ❸
MORNING
Begin the day at the **Bird Garden** *(see p93)*, then wind south through Kowloon's fascinating markets to traditional stores along **Shanghai Street** *(see p95)*.
AFTERNOON
Explore the shops along **Nathan Road** *(see p43)*, taking tea at **The Peninsula** *(see p85)*. Watch A Symphony of Lights from the **Waterfront Promenade** *(see p88)*, then head back to **Temple Street Night Market** *(see p22–3)* to pick up some souvenirs, as well as food for dinner.

Day ❹
ALL DAY
Spend a full day either exploring **Lantau Island** *(see pp116–17)* or indulging in fusion street food in **Macau** *(see pp122–9)*, and the evening at **Happy Valley Racecourse** *(see p16–17)*, hanging out with the locals. End your day at the lively bars in **Lan Kwai Fong** *(see p66)*.

Top 10 Hong Kong Highlights

Big Buddha and Po Lin Monastery, Lantau Island

TOP 10 Hong Kong Highlights

From opium port to Cold War enclave to frenetic financial capital, Hong Kong is steeped in history. East meets West in high style here, and the results amaze and delight. Prepare to experience one of the world's most dramatic urban environments.

1 The Peak
Take the tram to the lofty heights of Victoria Peak for an amazing view of the city skyline *(see pp12–13)*.

2 Central's Statue Square
Hong Kong Island's northwest is the region's administrative centre. Colonial remnants and modern architecture stand side by side on Statue Square *(see pp14–15)*.

3 Happy Valley Racecourse
Thrilling horse races and mid-week partying: Happy Valley Racecourse is where Hong Kongers come to play *(see pp16–17)*.

4 Star Ferry
Ignore the subterranean road and rail links between Hong Kong Island and Kowloon. The thrilling way to cross the water is on the Star Ferry *(see pp18–19)*.

Mai Po
Yuen Long
Ngar Hom Sha
Pat Heung
Lam Tei
Ma On Kong
NEW
Pak Long
Tuen Mun
Tai Lam Chung Reservoir
Tsuen Wa
So Kwun Tan
Chek Lap Kok
Discovery Bay
Tung Chung
10
Lantau Island
Mui Wo
Tong Fuk
West Lamma Channel

0 km   5
0 miles 5

9
Cheung Chau Island

Stanley (5)

An old fort steeped in colonial history and reminders of World War II, Stanley is a peaceful diversion from the frenetic city *(see pp20–21)*.

(6) Temple Street Night Market

Kowloon is at its most atmospheric at night. Head up the peninsula to the narrow lanes of Yau Ma Tei for serious haggling *(see pp22–3)*.

(7) Heritage Museum

Near Sha Tin in the New Territories, this Hong Kong museum is a must-see. Splendid high-tech audio-visual displays cover the region's cultural heritage and natural history *(see pp26–7)*.

Tai Long Wan Coastline (8)

The remote, rugged Sai Kung Peninsula in the New Territories is the place to find Hong Kong's finest beaches *(see pp28–9)*.

Cheung Chau Island (9)

Of the several islands around Hong Kong, tiny Cheung Chau is arguably the loveliest, with traces of old China *(see pp30–31)*.

(10) Big Buddha and Po Lin Monastery

Visible from miles away, the Big Buddha is a major tourist destination *(see pp32–3)*.

TOP 10 ★ The Peak

With Hong Kong's most spectacular views, cooler climes and quiet wooded walks, it's no wonder Victoria Peak is so popular among the city's most affluent residents, who occupy the exclusive properties dotting its slopes. The Peak Tram takes under 10 minutes to reach Victoria Gap, pinning you to your seat as it's hauled up the sheer slope at the end of a single cable (don't worry, its safety record is spotless).

1 Peak Tower

The Peak Tram empties into an anvil-shaped mall **(above)** that houses shops and restaurants, as well as the Sky Terrace 428 viewing gallery. Standing at 428 m (1,404 ft), this is the highest viewing platform in a city full of vertiginous observation points. Children will enjoy Madame Tussaud's waxworks inside the tower in particular.

2 One of the World's Most Expensive Streets

Pollock's Path, on the Peak, earned this title in 2013, owing to properties being sold here regularly for over US$100 million. In 2017, an especially ritzy estate went for a record-breaking US$360 million.

3 Galleria

Although the imposing Peak Tower mall is hardly sensitive to its grand setting, there is a good range of places to eat and drink inside its Galleria, with great views down onto the city and harbour, and across to Lamma Island.

4 Barker and Plantation Roads

These usually quiet (although pavement-free) roads are worth wandering for a peep at some of the Peak's more expensive properties. Most of them have amazing harbour views. Enjoy a tranquil walk along the meandering path, starting at dawn to catch the sunrise.

5 The Peak Lookout

This much-loved, upmarket drinking and dining spot has a fine terrace, great food, an excellent wine list and friendly ambience.

6 Pok Fu Lam Country Park

For a gentle half-hour ramble, head down Pok Fu Lam Reservoir Road, then catch a bus back into town **(below)**.

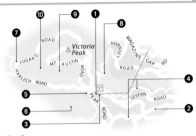

The Peak

9 Victoria Peak Garden

The steep struggle up Mount Austin Road to these gardens is worth the effort for the amazing spectacle at the top. The viewing platform looks across the channel to Lamma Island.

10 View Near Summit

The summit itself is fenced off and covered by telecom masts, but the views **(left)** from the edges of Victoria Peak Garden are excellent.

THE PEAK TRAM

Despite the fact that a single steel cable hauls the tram up a long and incredibly steep track, the Peak Tram has had a faultless safety record since the service opened in 1888. The most severe disruption to services came in the 1960s when torrents of water from a violent storm washed away part of the track.

NEED TO KNOW

MAP E5 ■ 2522 0922 ■ Bus 15C from Central Star Ferry ■ www.the peak.com.hk

Peak Tram: open 7am–midnight daily; adm

Sky Terrace 428: open 10am–8pm Mon–Fri, 8am–8pm Sat & Sun; adm HK$52

■ A joint pass for Peak Tram and Sky Terrace 428 is available (single/return HK$85/$99).

■ If it is misty or there's low cloud, delay your visit as you'll miss the excellent views.

■ Avoid taking the tram on weekends and public holidays as the queues can be extremely long.

■ The Peak Tower has some superb places to eat, from casual spots to signature restaurants.

7 Lugard and Harlech Roads

The effortless way to see most of the best views on offer from the Peak is on the shaded, well-paved, 3 km (2 mile) circular walk along Lugard Road and Harlech Road. It also makes for a terrific jogging track with a tremendous view **(above)**.

8 Old Peak Road

This former footpath up the Peak, created before the Peak Tram arrived, is pleasant and shaded. Surfaced, but incredibly steep, it is best saved for a descent. Take a detour onto Tregunter Path near the bottom to avoid the traffic.

👑🔟 ⭐ Central's Statue Square

Stand in Central district's Statue Square and you're right in the region's financial, political, historical and social heart. Peppered around the area, amid the steel and glass of the sleek modern skyscrapers, are a few colonial remnants, including the Neo-Classical Court of Final Appeal, outside which many political demonstrations have taken place. Shopping, which has long been a popular Hong Kong pursuit, can be enjoyed in the numerous swanky boutiques located on the opposite side.

Chater Garden ③

Despite the prime real-estate value of its site, on what was once the pitch of the Hong Kong Cricket Club, the small but well-tended Chater Garden **(right)** sprang up instead of a skyscraper. It's free to enter and makes for a good place to enjoy a cold drink and rest tired legs.

① Bank of China Tower

Looming over the HSBC building, the 72-storey Bank of China Tower **(above)** is perhaps the most iconic building on the downtown skyline. Renowned architect I M Pei designed the dizzying tower, allegedly using feng shui to help the bank *(see p38)* dominate the financial district.

② Thomas Jackson Statue

One of Hong Kong's few remaining statues, of a 19th-century banker, is in Statue Square. The Japanese army removed one of Queen Victoria, which gave the square its name.

④ Shopping Malls

Two of Hong Kong's most upmarket shopping malls – the busy Landmark Centre and the less busy Prince's Building *(see p69)* – sit next to Statue Square. Both are home to many luxurious and elegant boutiques, including Armani, Gucci and Prada.

⑤ The Cenotaph

Standing at the northern edge of Statue Square, the Cenotaph **(below)** is a memorial to those who died in the two world wars.

NEED TO KNOW

MAP L5

■ For a terrific bird's-eye view over Central and the harbour, head over to the HKMA Information Centre on the 55th floor of Two IFC Tower *(see pp38–9)*. Or, try the wraparound terrace at Sevva bar and restaurant *(see p70)*.

■ If you fancy picnicking in the square or in the nearby Chater Garden, try the fantastic pastries, cakes and quiches from the Mandarin Oriental's Cake Shop *(2825 4008)*, which is at the edge of the square.

6 Mandarin Oriental

At only 91 m (298 ft), it's hard to believe, but the Mandarin Oriental *(see pp148–9)* was once Hong Kong's tallest building. Today its graceful exterior seems overwhelmed by the ceaseless traffic, but inside it's still one of Hong Kong's finest hotels.

DEMOCRACY'S TRICKY PATH

During the Handover negotiations *(see p37)*, China was adamant that Hong Kong's Legislative Council would be just as democratic under Chinese rule as it was under the British (in other words, it could be argued, hardly at all). When Chris Patten, the last governor, tried to introduce greater representation, the mainland press called him "a serpent".

9 Former French Mission

Behind the HSBC building, this handsome mid-19th-century red-brick edifice has served as a French Catholic mission, Hong Kong's first Government House and, until 2015, the Court of Final Appeal.

7 HSBC Bank Headquarters

On its completion in 1985, Norman Foster's bold building was the most expensive ever built, costing more than HK$5bn. The edifice is said to have the strongest feng shui in Hong Kong. Rubbing the paws of the bank's handsome lions is said to bring good luck.

Central's Statue Square

8 Rest Day

Hundreds of domestic workers enjoying their day off on Sunday gather in public spaces like the pedestrian bridges, underpasses and streets throughout Central.

10 Court of Final Appeal

This Neo-Classical building **(above)** – a rare survivor from the city's colonial period – housed the Legislative Council, Hong Kong's equivalent to a parliament. The Court of Final Appeal moved here in 2015.

Happy Valley Racecourse

Feel the earth move beneath thundering hooves as you cheer the finishers home in the ultimate Hong Kong night out. Races have been held at Happy Valley – the widest stretch of flat land on Hong Kong Island, originally a swamp – since 1846. Today, the action takes place beneath twinkling high-rises, forming a backdrop to nights spent enjoying live music and festivities held here.

1 Wednesday Night Races
The most exciting scheduled races **(below)** usually take place on Wednesday evenings. For the full atmosphere, jump on a Happy Valley-bound tram and bone up on the form in the Wednesday *Racing Post* on the way. Races are from 7:15pm to 11pm.

2 Happy Wednesday
Thanks to a plethora of bars and restaurants located at the racecourse, Wednesday nights here have become popular for mid-week partying. Entertainment here includes live music, DJs and street performers.

3 Racing Museum
This small museum **(below)** details Hong Kong's racing history and has a selection of art. Here, visitors can learn the story of the old trade in prized Mongolian and Chinese ponies. Note that it is closed during race meetings.

Happy Valley Racecourse

BE RESPONSIBLE

Bets are placed at the counters at the back of each floor of the main stand. If you choose to bet, accept the odds and avoid trying to win back any losses.

4 View from Moon Koon
For a fantastic track-side view, go to Moon Koon Restaurant. Racing and dining packages are available.

5 Come Horseracing Tour
Splendid Tours and Grey Line (see p146) both run this tour during scheduled race meetings. Tours entail entry to the Members' Enclosure, a welcome drink, a meal and guide service.

6 Silver Lining Skeleton

Silver Lining, Hong Kong's most famous horse, was the first to win more than HK$1 million. The equine skeleton takes pride of place in a glass cabinet at the Racing Museum.

8 The Crowd

Happy Valley has a 55,000 capacity (above), but is so popular that it sometimes sells out before the day. The enthusiasm among the punters is infectious. Stand in the open next to the track, for the best atmosphere.

9 Live Music

It might be known for its races, but many locals come for the live music. The racecourse's resident band, Carnivale, gets everyone partying. Book a table at the bar and let the band serenade you with covers of hit songs and their own originals.

10 Themed Nights

The racecourse often hosts themed nights for visitors to join in on the holiday fun, whether it's St Patrick's Day or Chinese New Year. Expect food, performances and a fantastic evening.

7 Jockey Club Booths

For help and advice on placing bets go to the friendly Jockey Club officials (below) at the booths between the main entrance and the racetrack. The Jockey Club is the only organization allowed to take bets in Hong Kong. The tax it collects makes up a small but significant percentage of government revenue, but is being threatened by illegal and online betting.

NEED TO KNOW

MAP P6 ■ Less than 1 km (0.5 miles) south of Causeway Bay on Hong Kong Island ■ Dial 1817 for race details ■ Meets Wed, and occasionally, Sat & Sun (Sep–Jul) ■ Adm HK$10 ■ www. hkjc.com; www.happyvalleyrace course.com

Racing Museum: 2966 8065; open noon–7pm daily (noon–9pm on race days)

Come Horseracing Tour: 2368 7111; adm HK$1180; www.splendid.hk

■ A Tourist badge, available with a passport at the Badge Inquiry Office, gives you access to the member's enclosure.

■ Moon Koon Restaurant (*2966 7111; open noon–3pm & 6:30–10:30pm daily; www.hkjc.com*), on the second floor of the main stand, offers Chinese food. Advance booking needed on race nights.

TOP 10 ★ Star Ferry

One of Hong Kong's best-loved institutions, the Star Ferries have shuttled people between Kowloon and Hong Kong Island since 1888. They are still used by commuters despite the advent of rail and road tunnels beneath the harbour. A ferry ride offers a thrilling perspective on the towering skyscrapers and the jungle-clad hills of Hong Kong Island. Take an evening voyage for the harbour's daily neon spectacle, A Symphony of Lights, when 47 buildings on both sides of the harbour put on a light and sound show.

1 The Fleet
In the early days, four coal-fired boats went back and forth between Hong Kong and Kowloon. Today, 8 diesel-powered vessels **(below)** operate, each named after a particular star (with the night-time glare and pollution, the only stars you're likely to see from the harbour).

2 Clock Tower
Standing next to the Tsim Sha Tsui Star Ferry, the land-mark clock tower **(left)** is the last remnant of the old Kowloon railway terminus completed in 1915. Until 1975, this was the poetic final stop for trains arriving from the mainland.

3 Star Ferry Crew
Many Star Ferry crew members still sport old-fashioned uniforms, keeping tradition alive. Watch out, too, for the crewmen catching the mooring rope with a long billhook.

4 Skyline South
As you cross Victoria Harbour from Kowloon, on the far left you'll see the glass and flowing lines of the Convention Centre **(above)** in Wan Chai and above it the 373-m (1,223-ft) tower of Central Plaza. Further right are the Bank of China's striking zig-zags, and the HSBC building. However, the real giant is Two IFC *(see pp38–9)*, once the Island's tallest skyscraper.

5 Hong Kong Maritime Museum

Opened in 2013, this museum **(above)** explores the vast maritime history and trade of the Pearl River Delta, from the Song Dynasty through to the present day, as well as the marine life of the South China Sea.

9 Ocean Terminal

Just north of the Tsim Sha Tsui terminal, Hong Kong's cruise ships dock, including the world's most famous liners **(below)**. Some US warships also moor here during port calls.

NEED TO KNOW

MAP L4 ▪ 2367 7065 ▪ Ferries TST to Wan Chai: 7:20am–10:50pm daily; TST to Central: 6:30am–11:30pm daily ▪ www.starferry.com.hk

A Symphony of Lights: 8pm daily; www.tourism.gov.hk/symphony

Hong Kong Maritime Museum: Central Pier No. 8; 3713 2500; open 9:30am–5:30pm Mon–Fri, 10am–7pm Sat, Sun & public hols; www.hkmaritimemuseum.org

▪ The Hong Kong Tourism Board (HKTB) office *(open 8am–8pm daily)* in the Tsim Sha Tsui Star Ferry building is the most convenient place to pick up brochures, get help and advice, as well as buy Star Ferry models and other souvenirs.

---

6 Star Ferry Routes

The ferries operate daily between Tsim Sha Tsui and Central every 6 to 12 minutes, and between Tsim Sha Tsui and Wan Chai every 8 to 20 minutes.

7 Sightseeing Bargain

With fares ranging from just HK$2.60 to HK$4.20, a crossing on a Star Ferry is one of Hong Kong's best sightseeing bargains.

8 Tours

Star Ferries run several afternoon and evening ferry tours of the harbour on their "Shining Star" ferry, which is more comfortable than the regular ferry. The Shining Star ferry has an air-conditioned top deck as well as a café.

10 Skyline North

As you approach Kowloon **(below)**, you'll see the Arts and Cultural Centre closest to the shore. Behind it rises the grand extension of the Peninsula Hotel, with the huge ICC Tower gleaming to the west.

TOP 10 ⭐ Stanley

Originally a sleepy fishing haven, Stanley was the largest settlement on Hong Kong Island before the British took rule. The modern town, hugging the southern coast, still makes a peaceful, pleasant escape from the bustle of the city. Traffic is minimal, and the pace of life relaxed, with plenty of good places to eat, good beaches and a large market for well-priced clothing, silks and souvenirs. For the most part, Stanley represents the British colonial impact on Hong Kong, though older Chinese tradition is present at the Tin Hau Temple.

1 Pubs and Restaurants

One of Stanley's best attractions is its excellent range of restaurants and bars *(see p83)*, including Ocean Rock & Seafood Tapas **(above)**. A host of restaurants, serving cuisine from Italian to Vietnamese, line Stanley Main Road, facing the sea.

2 Old Police Station

The handsome structure was built in 1859 and is Hong Kong's oldest surviving police station. The Japanese used it as their headquarters during World War II. It is now a supermarket.

3 Murray House

Shifted here from its original site in Central to make way for the Bank of China Tower *(see p14)*, this allegedly haunted 1846 Neo-Classical relic now houses several restaurants **(below)**. Adjacent Blake Pier is the departure point for ferries to Aberdeen and remote Po Toi island *(see p119)*.

Hikers above Stanley

4 Waterfront

The pretty waterfront **(above)** makes for a pleasant promenade between the market area and Murray House. The harbour was once home to a busy fleet of junks and fishing boats, but is now largely empty.

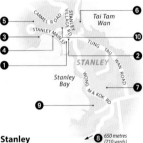

Stanley

5 Tin Hau Temple

This temple **(above)** is one of the oldest in Hong Kong. Lined with the statues of guards to the sea goddess Tin Hau, the interior of this 1767 temple is also one of the most evocative.

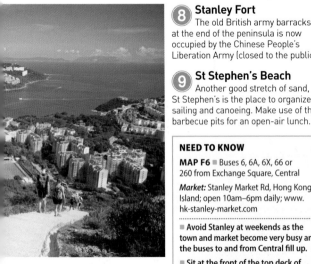

6 Stanley Beach

This fine stretch of sand is perfect for a dip and a paddle. It's the venue for the fiercely contested dragon boat races held in June *(see pp60–61)*.

7 Stanley Military Cemetery

Some of these graves belong to those who died during World War II. Others date back to early colonial days, when many succumbed to tropical illnesses.

THE WAR DEAD

After Japan overran Hong Kong in 1941 *(see p36)*, captured civilians suffered for three years under a regime of neglect and torture. Nine of those who died are buried at Stanley Military Cemetery.

8 Stanley Fort

The old British army barracks at the end of the peninsula is now occupied by the Chinese People's Liberation Army (closed to the public).

9 St Stephen's Beach

Another good stretch of sand, St Stephen's is the place to organize sailing and canoeing. Make use of the barbecue pits for an open-air lunch.

NEED TO KNOW

MAP F6 ■ Buses 6, 6A, 6X, 66 or 260 from Exchange Square, Central

Market: Stanley Market Rd, Hong Kong Island; open 10am–6pm daily; www. hk-stanley-market.com

■ Avoid Stanley at weekends as the town and market become very busy and the buses to and from Central fill up.

■ Sit at the front of the top deck of the bus to fully appreciate the dramatic coast road out to Stanley.

■ For alfresco dining, Ocean Rock & Seafood Tapas on Stanley's waterfront offers Spanish cuisine and delectable seafood, enjoyed with sea views.

10 Market

Reasonably priced clothes, shoes and accessories **(right)** as well as plenty of tourist tat are to be found among Stanley's pleasant market stalls *(see p57)*. Although it's not the cheapest market in Hong Kong, it's worth visiting before heading to one of the seafront restaurants.

🔟 ⭐ Temple Street Night Market

Beneath the bleaching glare of a thousand naked light bulbs, tourists and locals alike pick their way among the stalls crowding the narrow lanes of Yau Ma Tei's Temple Street. The overwhelming array of inexpensive goods includes clothes, shoes, accessories, designer fakes, copy CDs, bric-a-brac and souvenirs to take back home. Prices here may be a bit higher than in Shenzhen, just over the Chinese border, or in some of Hong Kong's less well-known markets, but Temple Street is unbeatable for atmosphere.

1 Fortune Tellers
Find out what your future holds – fortune tellers operate around the junction of Temple and Market streets. Most are face and palm readers. Look out for booths with signs in English.

2 Cantonese Opera Street Performers
Between 8:30pm and 11pm Thursday through Tuesday, singers and musicians perform popular Cantonese opera numbers **(below)**.

3 Dai Pai Dong
Redevelopment over the years has made *dai pai dong* food stalls a rare sight, but they are alive and well at Temple Street, selling a wide variety of Chinese snacks **(below)**, savoury pancakes, fishballs, seafood kebabs and unusual meat offerings.

Temple Street Night Market

4 Reclamation St Canteens
If you haven't had your fill from the *dai pai dong*, try the cheap noodles and rice dishes at the stalls on Reclamation Street. Don't mind your neighbour's table manners; it's customary to drop or spit gristle and bone onto the table-tops.

8 Watches

The watches sold here are likely to be a decent timekeeper but with no guarantee. The local makes and Western fakes are usually good value for money **(left)**. One stall offers genuine secondhand watches.

9 Clothes

Dig deep among the colourful market stalls to find good buys, including cheap T-shirts, silks **(right)**, beaded tops and cotton dresses. Have a look at the stall on the corner of Kansu Street.

5 Leather Goods

Leather is not really Temple Street's strong point. But belts are cheap, and there are plenty of leather bags and wallets, including attractive, fake Gucci, Elle and Burberry items. Some counterfeits for sale here may be more convincing than others.

HAGGLING

Remember, prices given are mostly starting points and the mark-ups are significant. The popularity of the market has driven prices up, so haggle hard (but do it with a smile), and remember the vendor is making a profit whatever price you both agree on. Begin below half the asking price and you should be able to get 50 per cent off most items.

6 Shoes

From the very cheap flip-flops to the reasonable suede or leather shoes, bargain footwear is available almost everywhere on Temple Street, although the variety is not huge and the styles not that elegant. A few stalls sell designer fakes.

10 Knick-knacks

Mao memorabilia, old posters, coins, opium pipes and jade are found on Public Square Street. Temple Street's north end is rich in kitsch plastic Japanese cartoon merchandise, including Afro Ken and Pokémon, and lucky *maneki-neko* cat figurines **(right)**.

7 Accessories

Cheap sunglasses **(below)** are easy to find. A variety of embroidered and beaded handbags, shoulder bags as well as jewellery are also worth looking out for.

NEED TO KNOW

MAP M1–2 ■ www.temple-street-night-market.hk

Open 4pm–midnight daily

■ Individual stall timings may vary, but the market really gets going after 7pm.

■ A good way to tackle the market is to start at the MTR to Yau Ma Tei (Exit C) and walk south from Portland Street, so that you end up near the bars and restaurants of Tsim Sha Tsui post shopping.

■ Buy a snack from the *dai pai dong* along the street.

TOP 10 ⭐ Heritage Museum

This modern museum, on the outskirts of Sha Tin in the New Territories, is one of Hong Kong's best. Opened in 2000, the Hong Kong Heritage Museum has six permanent galleries and six changing galleries covering the culture, arts and natural history of Hong Kong and the New Territories. Exciting audiovisual exhibits, a range of temporary exhibitions and a good interactive children's section make for a fun day out for visitors of all ages.

Architecture and Design

The Heritage Museum building (right) is based on the traditional Chinese *si he yuan* style, built around a courtyard. The style is still visible in the villages of the New Territories (see p110).

2 Orientation Theatre

For a brief overview of the museum, visit the Orientation Theatre on the ground floor opposite the ticket office.

3 Children's Discovery Gallery

The brightly coloured gallery (left) is a vibrant, fun way to introduce children to local nature and archaeology, and the history of toys. Interactive exhibits and the child-size 3D models are very popular with young children aged 4 to 10.

4 Cantonese Opera Heritage Hall

Cantonese opera is an obscure subject. However, the costumes (right), intricate stage settings and snatches of song from the elaborate operas of Guangdong and Guangxi on display in this gallery go some way towards illustrating this popular attraction.

NEED TO KNOW

MAP E3 ▪ 1 Man Lam Rd, Sha Tin, New Territories ▪ 2180 8188 ▪ MTR to Kowloon Tong, then bus 80M or MTR to Che Kung Temple, then a 5-minute walk ▪ www. heritagemuseum.gov.hk

Open 10am–6pm Mon, Wed–Fri, 10am–7pm Sat, Sun & public hols

Adm for special exhibitions (free for permanent exhibition)

▪ Combine a visit to the museum with a hike up the nearby Lion Rock (see p101) if you can.
▪ There is a small café and gift shop in the lobby.

Previous pages Central's skyscrapers from The Peak

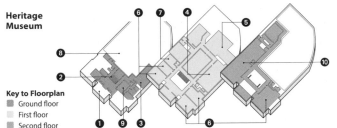

Heritage Museum

Key to Floorplan
- Ground floor
- First floor
- Second floor

6 Thematic Exhibitions

Six halls on the first and second floors house temporary exhibitions focusing on subjects varying from popular culture, contemporary art and social issues in Hong Kong, to traditional Chinese art and history.

7 Chao Shao-an Gallery

The delicate ink on scroll and porcelain paintings of artist and one-time Hong Kong resident Chao Shao-an are known far beyond China. There are dozens of fine examples on show in the gallery.

8 Courtyard

For fresh air and interesting surroundings, head to the shaded courtyard **(left)** in the centre of the complex.

9 Jin Yong Gallery

Dr Louis Cha (Jin Yong) was an influential martial arts novelist. The Jin Yong Gallery **(above)** explains his cultural impact and features exhibits on many of the movies and TV series based on his works.

10 TT Tsui Gallery of Chinese Art

The works of art dating from Neolithic times to the 20th century include porcelain, bronze, jade and stone artifacts, furniture, laquerware and religious statues **(below)**.

5 New Territories History

Examples of the rich fauna and flora of the region, along with 6,000-year-old artifacts from the early days of human habitation in Hong Kong, chart both the natural and social changes of the region.

HONG KONG'S EARLIEST SETTLERS

The New Territories History hall tells the scant story of Hong Kong's original inhabitants. Bronze Age people left behind axe and arrowheads in various parts of the territory more than 4,000 years ago, along with some mysterious rock carvings. Excavations on Lamma Island have turned up artifacts from an older Stone Age civilization, dating back about 6,000 years.

🔟⭐ Tai Long Wan Coastline

Although only 40 km (25 miles) from Hong Kong Island, the remote beaches on the eastern edge of the rugged Sai Kung Peninsula, in the New Territories, seem like another country. There is no rail link and few roads, so you will have to make an early start, taking at least two buses and an hour's walk to get to the first stretch of golden sands. The pristine coastline, glorious surf, delightful hidden pools and shaded cafés are worth every bit of the effort.

① Beaches
There are four excellent beaches at Tai Long Wan **(above)**. Tung Wan is the most remote and unspoiled; the smallest beach, Ham Tin, has a good café and camping area; Sai Wan Beach is the busiest.

③ Natural Swimming Pools
A lovely series of waterfalls and natural swimming pools **(left)** is the area's best-kept secret. These are accessed via the path running alongside the small river at the northwestern end of Tai Long Sai Wan beach.

② Beach Cafés
Noodles, fried rice and beverages can be found at the modest, reasonably priced cafés on Sai Wan Beach. Ham Tin also has some superb, though pricier, dining options.

④ Ham Tin to Tai Long Path
Take the steep 1-km (half-mile) path between Ham Tin and Sai Wan Beach for lovely views down onto Ham Tin, Tai Wan and the mountains behind **(below)**.

5 Surf Action

Tai Wan has reasonably good surf **(above)**. Bodyboarding should always be possible, and you may even be able to surf properly when storms raise bigger swells.

6 Pleasure Junks

Most privately hired junks drop anchor at Sai Wan Beach, and their passengers head to the beach in smaller craft, making this the busiest of the three beaches.

THE ROUTE OUT

A good route out of Tai Long Wan is the scenic path winding southwest from Sai Wan village around High Island Reservoir. Once you hit the main road outside Pak Tam Chung, there's a chance of picking up a bus or taxi back into Sai Kung town – but allow up to 5 hours walking just in case.

7 Hakka Fisherfolk

Tai Long village **(below)** may have been first settled in prehistoric times. It was a thriving Hakka fishing village until the 1950s, when most people migrated to the city or abroad. Only a few elderly residents remain in this sleepy place.

8 Campsite

The area just east of Ham Tin village is the best place for overnight campers; it has flat ground, barbecue pits, public toilets and a stream for fresh water. There are no hotels in the area.

9 Sharp Peak

The prominent 468-m (1,497-ft) summit of Sharp Peak is clearly visible from Ham Tin and Tai Wan. The arduous climb up its very steep slopes rewards visitors with some spectacular views over the peninsula.

10 Ham Tin Bridge

If you want to keep your feet dry, the only way to access the beach from Ham Tin village is via a small rickety bridge **(right)**. Marvel at its makeshift engineering, which features planks of driftwood and offcut material nailed together.

NEED TO KNOW

MAP H3 ■ MTR to Choi Hung, then minibus 1A to Sai Kung. From there, take a speedboat to the beaches, or taxi/minibus 29R to Sai Wan Pavilion

Daily junk hire from HK$5,500; visit the booths by the dock

■ Allow about 90 minutes from Kowloon or Central to the start of the path, plus at least an hour each way to hike to and from the beach.

■ Speedboats ply the route between Sai Kung Town and Sai Wan Beach or Ham Tin Beach (hourly until 5pm or 6pm; HK$120–160).

■ Beach cafés here offer a variety of local specialities. Some also rent out tents, sleeping bags and surfboards.

■ For picnic supplies, head to the well-stocked Wellcome supermarket located in Sai Kung.

Cheung Chau Island

This tiny, charming island, a half-hour high-speed ferry ride west of Hong Kong, makes a great escape from the heat and hassles of the city, (except maybe at weekends when everyone else has the same idea). The sense of an older, traditional Hong Kong is pervasive among the narrow streets, tiny shops and temples of this old pirate and fishing haven. It's possible to see most of the island in a day, taking it in with some lovely secluded walks. The seafood is cheap and there are small but excellent stretches of beach.

Pak Tai Temple ①
This highly decorative, renovated 1783 temple **(right)** is dedicated to Pak Tai, Cheung Chau's patron deity, who is credited with saving islanders from plague. The temple is the centre for the annual Bun Festival celebrations *(see p60)*, when mounds of buns are piled up to be offered to resident ghosts. The festival dates from the time of plagues in the 19th century, which were considered to be the vengeance of those killed by local pirates.

Harbour ②
Although Hong Kong's commerical fishing industry has dwindled from its heyday, plenty of fishing boats still operate from Cheung Chau's typhoon shelter harbour **(above)**. Cheap cycle hire is available along the waterfront.

Venerable Banyan Tree ③
On Tung Wan Road is an ancient tree **(below)** that is thought to be the source of Cheung Chau's good fortune. It is so revered by islanders that a restaurant opposite was knocked down instead of the tree to make way for a road.

PATHS AND WALKS

A footpath weaves around the southern edge of the island, taking in clifftop walks and a small Tin Hau Temple at Morning Beach. Heading southwest will take you along Peak Road past the cemetery to Sai Wan harbour. From here you can take a sampan shuttle back to the ferry pier.

Windsurfing Centre ④
The family of Olympic gold medallist Lee Lai-shan operates the windsurfing centre and café on Kwun Yam Beach.

Cheung Chau Island

5 "The Peak"

A walk up the hill along Don Bosco and Peak roads **(above)** will take you past some old colonial houses and lovely sea views. The cemetery on Peak Road has fine vistas.

6 Tung Wan Beach

The Cheung Chau Island's finest beach is on the east coast, located 150 m (500 ft) from the west coast's ferry pier. It is tended by lifeguards and also has a shark net.

7 Pirate's Cave

The place where 19th-century buccaneer Cheung Po-tsai supposedly stashed his booty, this "cave" is more of a hole or crevice **(right)**. Take a torch to explore. The sea views nearby make it worth the trip.

8 Boatbuilding Yard

At the harbour's northern end is a busy yard where junks are built and nets mended. Look out for the slabs of ice sliding along the overhead chute, down a mini helter-skelter and onto the boats.

9 Seafood Restaurants

If you want to dine on fish or shellfish, there's plenty of choice along the seafront on She Praya Road north and south of the ferry pier. The restaurants are cheaper than other seafood centres such as Lamma. Choose from the live tanks.

10 Ancient Rock Carving

In the Hong Kong region, there are several rock carvings **(left)** in close proximity to the sea. There are some near Tung Wan beach and Cheung Chau has one facing the sea. Nothing is known of the people who carved out these shapes about 3,000 years ago.

NEED TO KNOW

MAP C6 ■ Daily ferries hourly or half-hourly from Central Pier No. 5; high-speed ferries take just 35 minutes ■ www. nwff.com.hk

■ Hire bicycles (starting HK$50/day) from opposite the basketball courts close to Pak Tai Temple.

■ Cheung Chau's famous Bun Festival is held in early May, check www. hktb.com for dates.

■ Try Morocco's (2986 9767), by the ferry pier, which serves Indian, Thai and Western (but not Moroccan) fare in the evenings.

TOP 10 ⭐ Big Buddha and Po Lin Monastery

Once a humble house built in 1906 by three monks for worshipping the Buddha, Po Lin Monastery on Lantau Island is now a large and important temple. Its crowning glory, the giant Tian Tian Buddha statue facing the monastery, is an object of veneration for devotees and one of Hong Kong's most popular tourist sights. The statue dominates the area from a plinth reached by 268 steps. On a clear day, the view across the valleys, reservoirs and peaks of Lantau makes the climb more than worthwhile.

The Big Buddha **3**
Standing a lofty 34-m (112-ft) high, this mighty bronze statue **(right)** is among the largest seated Buddha images in the world. The statue, which was cast in more than 220 pieces, sits on a lotus throne – the Buddhist symbol of purity – and his right hand is raised, "imparting fearlessness".

1 Monastery
Attracted by its seclusion in Lantau's hills, Buddhist monks began arriving on Lantau in the early 20th century. The Po Lin or "precious lotus" monastery **(below)** developed as a place for pilgrimage in the 1920s when the Great Hall was built and the first abbot was appointed.

4 Ngong Ping 360 Cable Car
The cable-car ride *(see p49)* from Tung Chung to Po Lin is an attraction in itself **(below)**. The 4-mile (5.7-km), 25-minute journey provides sweeping views across the North Lantau Country Park and to the distant South China Sea.

2 Orchid Garden
Below the Big Buddha, near the Po Lin Hall, lies this beautiful garden where fragrant blossoms, planted all around the monastery, are cultivated.

(5) Great Hall

The main temple houses three large golden Buddha images **(above)**. Don't miss the ceiling paintings, the elaborate exterior friezes and the elegant lotus-shaped floor tiles.

(8) Fat Mun Ancient Path

Instead of taking the bus back, you can walk down to Tung Chung MTR via the lovely 4-mile- (7-km-) long Fat Mun Ancient Path, which runs along the wooded Tung Chung Valley. You'll pass smaller monasteries including Lo Hon, which serves vegetarian lunches and offers a serene spot for admiring the Tian Tan Buddha from a distance.

(9) Monks and Nuns

Robed, shaven-headed nuns and monks pray in the old temple behind the main one. Entry is forbidden to tourists visiting during the 3pm prayers.

(10) Temple Gateway

Guarded by a pair of ornate lion statues, the imposing temple gateway is said to replicate the southern gate to Buddhist heaven. As found elsewhere in the temple, traditional motifs such as reverse swastikas, which are the holy sign of Buddhism, adorn the gate. The Chinese characters at the top read "Po Lin Monastery".

(6) Bodhisattvas

On each side of the staircase are statues of Buddhist saints **(right)**. They are venerated for deferring heaven in order to help mortals reach enlightenment.

(7) Vegetarian Kitchen

The monastery's kitchen serves simple vegetarian meals to visitors from 11:30am to 4:30pm daily. They don't have an extensive menu, but the ingredients used are tasty, seasonal and fresh.

NEED TO KNOW

MAP B5 ■ MTR to Tung Chung, then No. 23 bus, or No. 2 bus from Lantau Island's Mui Wo ferry terminal; MTR to Tung Chung, then Ngong Ping 360 Cable Car to the village

The Big Buddha: open 10am–5:30pm daily; www.plm.org.hk

Monastery: open 8am–6pm daily

Ngong Ping 360 Cable Car: open 10am–6pm Mon–Fri, 9am–6:30pm Sat, Sun & public hols; adm single/return HK$160/$235; www.np360.com.hk

■ The YHA S G Davis Hostel *(2985 5610)* is ideal for viewing the sunrise from the summit of nearby Lantau Peak.

The Top 10
of Everything

**A traditional Chinese dragon used
in ceremonial dances**

TOP 10 Moments in History

1 5000 BC: Early Peoples

For many years, it was believed that Hong Kong was a "barren rock" devoid of people when the British arrived. However, archaeology shows that early ancestors of the She people had settled by the seaside on Hong Kong Island and the New Territories some six millennia ago. The area was loosely incorporated into China during the Qin Dynasty.

2 AD 1127: Local Clans

When the Mongols drove the Song dynasty emperor's family out of the imperial capital of Kaifeng, one princess escaped to the walled village of Kam Tin in the New Territories, where she married into the powerful Tang clan.

3 1841: The British Take Hong Kong Island

In a decisive move during the First Opium War (1839–42) between China and Britain, Captain Charles Elliot of the British Royal Navy landed on Hong Kong Island and planted the Union Jack flag on 25 January. The 8,000-odd Tanka fishermen and Hakka charcoal burners were largely unaffected, but China and Britain continued to fight over other Chinese trading cities. The 1842 Treaty of Nanking ceded Hong Kong Island to the British.

19th-century pirate

4 1898: The 99-Year Lease

Following earlier skirmishes between Britain and China, the colonial power dug in, turning Hong Kong into a mighty fort. Lyemun at the eastern end of the island bristled with guns and the world's first wire-guided torpedo. Breathing space and water supplies were assured when, on 1 July, the 99-year lease of the New Territories was signed in Beijing.

5 1941: Japanese Occupation

The Japanese, who arrived by land, had little trouble breaching the aptly named Gin Drinkers Line – a motley string of pillboxes. Hong Kong was surrendered two days before Christmas, beginning a brutal three-year occupation.

6 1950: Economic Miracle

Hong Kong's transformation into a manufacturing centre began when scores of refugees from across China crossed the border into the city, where they joined an already growing workforce and fuelled the economy.

Japanese soldiers captured by the British, 1945

7 1997: Handover

Following the Sino-British joint Declaration in 1984, when Deng Xiaoping promised to preserve Hong Kong's autonomy under "One Country, Two Systems", Britain handed Hong Kong back to China at midnight on 30 June 1997.

The Handover ceremony, 1997

8 1998: Financial Crisis

The financial crisis that had rocked other parts of Asia began to be felt in Hong Kong towards the end of 1997. Although it was not as badly hit as some countries, the financial crisis took its toll nonetheless.

9 2014: Umbrella Movement

After Beijing reneged on its promise to allow Hong Kong to democratically elect its leader, the city took to the streets. Protesters occupied major thoroughfares in a key financial district, camping out in tents for 79 days.

10 2019: Anti-Extradition Protests

A summer of protests ensued against a bill that would allow fugitives to be sent to mainland China for trial. The demonstrations morphed into a movement opposing Beijing's perceived overreach into Hong Kong. Protesters marched for freedom and occasionally clashed violently with police.

TOP 10 FIGURES IN HISTORY

1 Jorge Alvares
In 1513, a Portuguese navigator, Alvares became the first European to visit Hong Kong.

2 Cheung Po-tsai
The Lantau-based pirate king Cheung Po-tsai wreaked havoc, plundering international traders in 1810.

3 Lin Zexu
In 1839, Commissioner Lin Zexu was appointed by China with the task of ending the trade in imported opium.

4 Captain Charles Elliot
Flag-planter Captain Charles Elliot claimed Hong Kong Island for Britain and Queen Victoria in 1841.

5 Sir Henry Pottinger
Pottinger was the first governor of Hong Kong. He reportedly turned a blind eye to illicit shipments of opium.

6 Dr Sun Yat-sen
This reformer blasted China as "chaotic and corrupt" during a lecture at the University of Hong Kong in 1923. Economic boycott of the colony followed.

7 Rensuke Isogai
Infamous military commander, Isogai was a wartime governor of Hong Kong under Japanese occupation.

8 Deng Xiaoping
The Chinese premier, Deng Xiaoping stuck to his principles during Handover talks with Margaret Thatcher in 1984.

9 Chris Patten
The last British governor, Patten, waved goodbye to Hong Kong in 1997.

10 Tung Chee-hwa
The shipping magnate Tung Chee-hwa became the first Chief Executive of Hong Kong after the Handover.

Deng Xiaoping, Chinese premier

🔟 Modern Buildings

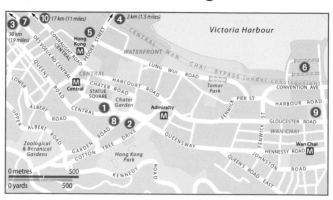

① HSBC Headquarters
MAP L5 ▪ 1 Queen's Rd Central, Central

Sir Norman Foster's striking, Blade Runner-esque edifice cost a whopping HK$5.2bn, making it the world's priciest building at the time when it opened in 1985. The headquarters of the Hong Kong and Shanghai Banking Corporation are reputed to have some of the best feng shui around – the building sits on a rare confluence of five "dragon lines" and enjoys unimpeded harbour views. The soaring atrium, filled with natural light, feels almost like a cathedral. Guarding the entrance is a pair of lion statues.

HSBC Headquarters atrium

② Bank of China Tower
MAP L6 ▪ 1 Garden Rd, Central

This one is also famous in feng shui circles, but more for dishing it out than possessing it – the glass-skinned tower *(see p14)* shoots bad vibes at the old Government House and other colonial entities. Its knife-like edges were the inspiration of the American-Chinese master architect I M Pei. The 70-storey, 367-m (1,205-ft) stack of prisms opened in 1990.

③ Hong Kong International Airport
MAP B4

Norman Foster's glass-dominated passenger terminal, which opened in July 1998, is impressive. The airport *(see p140)* is built on the flattened island of Chek Lap Kok.

④ International Commerce Centre (ICC)
MAP L2 ▪ 1 Austin Rd W, Kowloon ▪ Open 10am–9pm Sun–Thu, 10am–10:30pm Fri & Sat ▪ www.sky100.com.hk

With 108 storeys and at 484 m (1,588 ft), the ICC is Hong Kong's tallest building. It houses one of the world's highest hotels, the Ritz-Carlton, Hong Kong *(see p149)* and the sky100 Observation Deck.

⑤ Two IFC Tower
MAP L5 ▪ Exchange Square, Central ▪ 55/F HKMA Information Centre: open 10am–6pm Mon–Fri, 10am–1pm Sat ▪ www.hkma.gov.hk

The Two International Finance Centre Tower soars above Victoria

The majestic Two IFC Tower

Harbour. At 412 m (1,352 ft), it was Hong Kong's tallest building until it was overtaken by the International Commerce Centre in 2010. There is a large, upmarket shopping mall at its base. The Hong Kong Monetary Authority (HKMA) Information Centre offers spectacular views. Visitors are required to show a photo ID to enter.

6 HK Convention and Exhibition Centre

MAP N5 ■ 1 Expo Dr, Wan Chai

Site of the official Handover ceremony in 1997, the Centre sprawls across a huge area over the harbour and was designed to resemble a bird in flight.

7 Hong Kong-Zhuhai-Macau Bridge

MAP L–M6 ■ Lantau Island

The longest sea-crossing *(see p140)* on earth, this construction spans

55 km (34 miles) and comprises three bridges, three artificial islands and an undersea tunnel section.

8 Cheung Kong Centre

MAP L6 ■ 2 Queen's Rd Central, Central

Big, boxy and glassy, this building contains the office of business magnate Li Ka-shing. A crypto firm paid US$600,000 in rent for a lease in 2018, believed to be the priciest in the city.

9 Central Plaza

Confusingly, this is in Wan Chai, not Central *(see p73)*. With 78 storeys and at 374 m (1,227 ft) it is the third-tallest tower in Hong Kong. At night, the neon rods at top of the building change colour every 15 minutes.

10 Tsing Ma Bridge

MAP D4

The Tsing Ma double-decker suspension bridge stretches from Tsing Yi Island to Lantau. It is 2.2 km (1.5 miles) long and

Central Plaza

looks especially striking when lit up at night. It was opened in 1997 by former UK Prime Minister Margaret Thatcher, having taken five years to build at a cost of HK$7.14bn. Take the MTR to Tsing Yi or catch an airport bus to view it. There's also a viewing platform *(see p120)* at Ting Kau.

Tsing Ma Bridge at dusk, seen from Tsing Yi Island

![TOP 10] Cultural Experiences

1 Spend a Night at the Opera

www.cantoneseopera.hk

Cantonese opera is a fine and ancient art, combining song, mime, dancing, martial arts and fantastic costumes and make-up. The opera can go on for 6 hours or more. Contact the Tourist Board (see p145) for details of performances.

2 Feast on Dim Sum

Dim sum (see p53) is commonly translated as "touch the heart", and after a few plates of these delicious meat- or vegetable-filled dumplings, it is easy to see why. The steamed snacks are delivered on trolleys in bamboo baskets.

3 Ride on a Junk

Aqua Luna: tours depart from Tsim Sha Tsui Pier 1 & Central Pier 9; 2116 8821; www.aqualuna. com.hk ■ Dim Sum Cruise: 1–2:30pm daily ■ Afternoon Tea Cruise: 3–4:30pm daily ■ Evening Harbour Cruises: 5:30–9:30pm daily (hourly) ■ Adm

Hong Kong's junks – traditional boats with blood-red batwing sails–look spectacular as they glide over serene waters against the backdrop of Victoria Harbour, and promise an

Opera singer

exciting adventure. Hand built in the Hong Kong shipyard of an 80-year-old master craftsman, the *Aqua Luna* is one of the last remaining sailing junks.

4 Visit a Market

Hong Kong's wet markets (see pp56–7) offer up an exciting change from the order of the average grocery store. Wander through the street stalls, past fishmongers and butchers, as hawkers yell and locals bargain.

5 Go for a Traditional Tonic

MAP N6 ■ Cnr Luard and Lockhart Rds, Wan Chai

For a taste of the real China, try a bowl of tonic tea from a street-side stall. These bitter brews are concocted using herbs according to traditional Chinese medicinal principles of whether they are "cooling" or "heating". Royal Joy in Wan Chai labels all its offerings in English.

6 Try Foot Reflexology

Gao's Foot Massage: 17/F Silver Fortune Plaza, 1 Wellington St, Lan Kwai Fong; 2810 9219

Vice-like hands seek out pressure points linked to vital organs. The procedure might be painful, but you will feel relaxed and revitalized at the end of the treatment. Gao's Foot Massage parlour is an excellent option.

7 Experience Unbelievable Gall

MAP K5 ■ 13 Hillier St, Sheung Wan ■ 2543 8032

She Wong Lam in the northwest of Hong Kong Island is the best place to sup on snake wine, a traditional

Traditional junk, Victoria Harbour

winter tonic. The speciality is a fiery brew containing the gallbladders of five deadly snakes.

Practice Tai Chi
MAP M4

Turn up at Avenue of the Stars (see p86) in front of the Museum of Art in Tsim Sha Tsui at 8am on Mondays, Wednesdays and Fridays to enjoy an insightful hour-long instruction in this gentlest of martial arts.

Chi Lin Nunnery, Kowloon

Aim for Everything Zen

For a modern take on ancient China, check out the Chi Lin Nunnery in Kowloon. This gorgeous replica of a seven-hall Tang dynasty (AD 618–907) complex took 10 years to build, using traditional techniques and materials. Bliss out listening to the nuns chanting to the Sakyamuni Buddha (see p102).

10 Watch a Lion Dance

Lions are thought to ward off evil and bring luck, which explains why the opening of a new building often features a fascinating display of youths dancing beneath a stylized lion's head. These performances are commonly seen around Chinese New Year (see p60).

Lion dance

(see p86)

TOP 10 SPA EXPERIENCES

Relaxing Peninsula Spa

1 Peninsula Spa
2696 6682
Check into the Peninsula (see p149) for a relaxing retreat at the luxurious spa.

2 The Ritz-Carlton Spa
1 Austin Rd ▪ 2263 2040
Go for a deep-tissue Chinese massage and get the blood circulating.

3 The Bliss Spa
1 Austin Rd ▪ 3717 2797
This spa at W Hong Kong offers a range of treatments.

4 The Mandarin Barber
5 Connaught Rd Central ▪ 2825 4088
A Shanghai-style shave at the Mandarin Oriental will leave your face feeling fresh and smooth.

5 Chinese Traditional Medicine
Boost your staying power with a tonic drink from one of the many kerbside Chinese medicine shops.

6 Raymond Lo
www.raymond-lo.com
Set your house and garden in tune with the elements with a private feng shui consultation.

7 Perfect Pointe Physiotherapy
30–32 Connaught Rd Central ▪ 2522 0168
Relieve yourself of any travelling aches with an acupuncture session.

8 Immortelle Divine Secret
9 Star St, Wan Chai ▪ 2143 6288
The 45-minute detox warming body wrap at the Spa L'Occitane is divine.

9 The Mandarin Spa
5 Connaught Rd Central ▪ 2825 4888
Fans rave about the traditional Shanghai pedicure from the spa at the Mandarin Oriental (see pp148–9).

10 Health Wise Chinese Medicine
Dr Troy Sing ▪ 2526 7908
Try some alternative medicine from a traditional Chinese doctor.

🔟 Walking Routes and Promenades

The skyscrapers of Central as seen from the Peak Circuit

1 The Peak Circuit

This loop around Victoria Peak (see pp12–13) takes about an hour to complete at a gentle pace. Formed by Harlech and Lugard roads, the circuit offers jaw-dropping city panoramas to the north, boundless sea views to the south, and glimpses of the many millionaires' homes among the greenery en route.

2 Temple Street Night Market

Allow plenty of time, not for the distance (Temple Street is no more than half a mile end to end), but to explore the pageantry of hawker stalls, fortune tellers, medicine men and opera singers that set up along here (see pp22–3) every night.

3 The MacLehose Trail

MAP G3

It spans over 100 km (60 miles) across the New Territories, so only bona fide outdoor types will attempt the whole length. But certain sections are

easily accessible (try the lovely part around the High Island Reservoir) for visitors who value the prospect of being back at the hotel bar by nightfall. Information can be found on the HKTB website (see p145).

4 Central to Western via Hollywood Road

Central's futuristic office towers and concrete canyons give way to the low-rise charm of antique shops, galleries and bars the further west you go, ending up in Western's archetypal Chinese shopping streets and docksides (see pp64–7). A must visit.

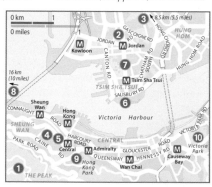

5 The Hong Kong Land Loop
MAP L5

Almost all of Central's prestigious commercial towers are part of the portfolio of one company, Hong Kong Land, which has thoughtfully connected its properties with aerial walkways. The buildings include Jardine House, Mandarin Oriental, Prince's Building and the Landmark. Do the circuit, if only for the ethereal experience of experiencing downtown Hong Kong without ever touching the ground.

6 Cultural Centre Promenade

This walkway from the Kowloon Star Ferry, past the InterContinental, is notable for great views of Hong Kong Island's towers. See these lit to music nightly at 8pm in A Symphony of Lights *(see p88)*.

7 Nathan Road

Often called the Golden Mile, this famed shopping strip runs up the Kowloon peninsula, passing hotels and tourist shops at the upscale southern end. Keep going to pass neon-lit karaoke lounges and low-rent storefronts of central Kowloon. Well-priced electronics stores dot the road, should a bargain be of fancy *(see p85)*. If you need respite from the hectic street life, stop off at Kowloon Park *(see p87)*.

Fishing boats at Cheung Chau

8 The Praya, Cheung Chau

The *praya* (or waterfront road) of Cheung Chau Island *(see pp30–31)* is everything the main drag of a backwater fishing town should be: a rambling tableau of fresh catches, boats tying up, market stalls and skipping kids. Look out for the splendid hand-pulled water carts that are the island's only fire engines.

9 The Central Green Trail
MAP L6

Just minutes from the towering banks, malls and offices of downtown, this signposted, hour-long trail from the Peak Tram terminus at Hong Kong Park opens up a lush hillside world of trees, ferns and rocks. A beautiful, shady walk that offers an alternative to taking the tram to the top.

10 Victoria Park

One of the city's larger green sites, Victoria Park *(see p74)* is best visited in the early morning, when tai chi devotees exercise and it is at its most peaceful. Throughout the day there are people-watching opportunities and restful walks, away from the urban bustle.

Neon signs on Nathan Road

 Areas of Natural Beauty

Sea birds at Mai Po Nature Reserve

1 Cape D'Aguilar
MAP F6

It may be only 11 km (7 miles) directly south of Hong Kong's busy Central district, but Cape D'Aguilar feels like another world. The wild coastline has wave-lashed rock formations and a marine life so rich that researchers have discovered 20 new species in its waters.

2 Hoi Ha Wan
MAP G2

The long inlets and sheltered coves of this marine park in northern Sai Kung are made for snorkelling. The waters here are replete with stony coral and visitors can spot diverse species of colourful reef fish.

3 Mai Po Nature Reserve

Declared a Ramsar site (a wetland of international importance) in 1995, Mai Po (see p111) is one of China's major bird sanctuaries, with hundreds of resident and migratory species recorded here, including many endangered ones. Other wildlife that thrive here include otters, civet cats, bats and amphibians. Tours are organized by WWF on weekends.

4 Bride's Pool

The scenic pool (see p111) is a popular picnic spot. Weekends are best avoided, but visit midweek and, with some luck, you will have this glorious, wooded course of rockpools and cascades all to yourself.

5 Pat Sin Leng Country Park
MAP F2

Hong Kong's countryside is home to the empty valleys and sublime uplands of Pat Sin ("eight spirits"). Peaks range up to 639 m (2,095 ft), and the views are humbling.

6 Three Fathom's Cove
MAP G3

Take steep steps up the rock from Three Fathom's Cove, and enter an expanse of remote uplands and boulder-strewn paths, leading, in the north, to Horse Tail Ridge. There are exquisite views of the Tolo Channel to be enjoyed from here.

7 Sha Lo Tung
MAP F2

This hidden valley in the New Territories is probably the closest Hong Kong comes to the stereotypical idea of a classical Chinese landscape, with its old paddy fields, deserted villages, flowing streams and ancient woods. It is magical.

White sand beaches of Tai Long Wan

Walkers on the Dragon's Back

8 Dragon's Back
MAP F5

This undulating ridge snakes down Hong Kong Island's south-east corner, with plunging slopes, poetic sea views and (past Pottinger's Gap) deep wooded valleys and beaches.

9 Tai Long Wan

On the Sai Kung Peninsula, survive the knuckle-whitening ascent of Sharp Peak (all loose rocks and narrow paths), and the land plunges down to your well-earned reward: the sparkling waves and white sand beaches of Hong Kong's finest bay, Tai Long Wan (see pp28–9).

10 Ma On Shan

Plateaus and grassy slopes surround the Ma On Shan peak (see p111), whose name literally means "Saddle Mountain" due to its shape. These sites offer panoramic views of the mountainous countryside, without the insidious intrusion of city skyline in the distance. The effect is truly majestic and worth the climb.

The peak of Ma On Shan

🔟 Off the Beaten Track

Mandarin's House in Largo do Lilau, Macau

1 Largo do Lilau, Macau
Mandarin's House: 10 Travessa de António da Silva; open 10am–6pm Mon, Tue & Thu–Sun; www.wh.mo/mandarinhouse/en

This tiny cobbled square was one of the earliest districts settled by Portuguese, and there's a distinctly European flavour to the surrounding shuttered windows and stuccoed façades. Head to the beautifully restored 19th-century Mandarin's House nearby for a taste of Classical Chinese architecture.

2 Pineapple Dam
MAP E4

This is also known as Shing Mun Reservoir. There's an easy 2-hour walk here through the woodland around the water, with the chance to see macaques and birds. Bring lunch and make use of the barbecue sites, or extend your hike to Tai Mo Shan or Tai Po town.

3 Sham Chung Tsuen
MAP G2

An abandoned 18th-century Hakka village, Sham Chung Tsuen is set next to the Sham Chung ferry pier. It is a great place to spend an afternoon exploring old houses shrouded in vegetation. One of the houses is open on weekends and serves snacks.

4 Hong Kong Cemetery
MAP F5 ■ Wong Nai Chung Rd, Causeway Bay ■ Open 7am–6pm daily (until 7pm Apr–Oct)

Rising in terraces up the hillside opposite the racetrack, these cemeteries provide a snapshot

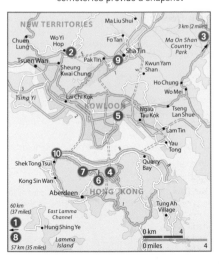

Historic Hong Kong Cemetery

of the people including Muslims, Christians, Parsis and Jews, who once settled this busy outpost. The Protestant section is the most atmospheric, overgrown with trees and crowded with Victorian-era mausoleums.

5 Sung Wong Toi
MAP E4 ■ Ma Tau Chung Rd, Kowloon City

Though lacking in drama, Sung Wong Toi is a rare reminder that Hong Kong history far predates the British arrival in 1842. This boulder is the sole surviving fragment of a terrace once frequented by the last Song dynasty prince, who fled here to escape the 12th-century Mongol invasion of China.

6 Bowen Road
MAP E5

A short but bracing walk uphill from busy Queens Road East in Wan Chai, Bowen Road is a narrow concrete strip that runs through unexpectedly thick forest, where traffic noise from below mingles with the humming of cicadas. Lovers' Rock, a phallic-shaped boulder poking rudely up through the treeline here, is a focus for the Maidens' Festival in August.

7 Nam Koo Terrace
MAP M6 ■ 55 Ship St, Wan Chai

Reputedly the most haunted place in Hong Kong, this spooky, uninhabited, mouldering old Chinese mansion sits uncomfortably in the shadows of Wan Chai's towering skyscrapers, draped in strangler figs and the stalking grounds for an unlikely number of feral cats. Though a protected building, redevelopment plans are a real threat.

8 Three Lamps District
A bustling market area in the back lanes of northern Macau. Lanes radiating out from the Rotunda de Carlos da Maia are choked by stalls selling clothing, vegetables and all manner of daily necessities. On the periphery are some low-key temples and the Art Deco façade of the Red Market, where you can buy live meat for the cooking pot.

9 Tsang Tai Uk
This small, old, Hakka clan mansion (see p110) is strangely overlooked by visitors, despite being an easy walk from Sha Tin's Heritage Museum. Built by the Tsang family between the 1840s and the 1860s, the complex is well-preserved, with fortress-like walls and protective "tiger-fork" spikes on the roofs. Parts are still lived in today by dozens of families.

10 Lo Pan Temple
MAP E5 ■ 15 Ching Lin Terrace, Kennedy Town ■ 2802 2880

A short walk uphill from the Belcher's Bay Park tram stop, this small temple dates from 1884 and is the only one in Hong Kong dedicated to Lo Pan, the patron deity of carpenters. The two halls sport a gorgeous, ornate roof, decorated with figures made at the famous ceramics centre of Shiwan, in China.

Lo Pan Temple

TOP 10 Children's Attractions

Exhibit at the Science Museum

1 Science Museum
Several hands-on exhibits and fascinating displays at this museum *(see p86)* provide a fun and educational introduction to many facets of science. Any child with a healthy dose of curiosity will spend hours pushing buttons, pulling levers and marvelling at gadgets.

2 Ocean Park
"Connecting people with nature" is what it's all about at Ocean Park *(see p79)*. The Giant Panda Habitat and the marine Atoll Reef and Sea Jelly Spectacular exhibits will keep children engrossed for hours. The park also features tons of exciting rides, plus a cable car

Parade at Disneyland

overlooking the southern peaks of Hong Kong Island. Families can take advantage of the park's glamping experience.

3 Zoological and Botanical Gardens
MAP K6 ▪ Albany Rd, Central ▪ Open 6am–7pm daily ▪ www. lcsd.gov.hk/en/parks/hkzbg

A modicum of Victorian gentility survives in the wrought-iron bandstand and shrub-lined paths of this delightful park founded in 1864. A little oasis of calm, it features pretty gardens, a children's play area and an aviary with 280 species of birds which kids are sure to love.

4 Hong Kong Disneyland
MAP C4 ▪ Lantau Island ▪ 1-830-830 ▪ Adm ▪ www.hongkongdisneyland.com

Located on the eastern edge of Lantau Island, Disneyland has its own MTR station. Designers wisely used feng shui in the layout of the park, and there are a few nods to local culture too. The themed areas – Fantasyland Adventureland, and Tomorrowland – lie beyond Main Street, USA.

The Dragon rollercoaster at Ocean Park

Ngong Ping 360 Cable Car

⑤ Ngong Ping 360 Cable Car

The spectacular 25-minute cable-car journey offers an escape from the hustle and bustle of the city. Moving across open water and up the steep hillside from Tung Chung to the Big Buddha at Po Lin (see pp32–3), this is the best ride in town (see p120).

⑥ Dolphin Watching

MAP B4 ■ 2984 1414 ■ Bus pick-up 8:50am at Kowloon Hotel or boat pick-up 9:25am at Tung Chung New Development Pier, Lantau ■ Open Wed, Fri, Sun ■ Adm ■ www. hkdolphinwatch.com

Hong Kong's waters are home to the rare Indo-Pacific hump-back dolphins, which here in the Pearl River delta are a pale-pink colour. Try your luck at spotting these beautiful creatures.

⑦ Lions Nature Education Centre

MAP G3 ■ Tsiu Hang, Sai Kung, New Territories ■ 2792 2234 ■ Open 9:30am–4:30pm Wed–Mon ■ www.afcd.gov.hk

The Lions Nature Education Centre is more fun than it sounds, with fruit orchards, an arboretum, rock gardens and an insectarium. The Centre promotes nature education, field studies and ecotours for schools, organizations and the public.

⑧ Tram Tour

Rock, rattle and roll along the front of Hong Kong Island, or take a detour around Happy Valley. Hong Kong's trams (see p141) may be slow, crowded and noisy, but they are terrific for sightseeing.

⑨ Kowloon Park

The green lungs of Tsim Sha Tsui (see p87) have a huge indoor-outdoor swimming pool, lots of gardens and children's favourite, the Avenue of Comic Stars featuring life-size statues.

Avenue of Comic Stars, Kowloon Park

⑩ Hong Kong Wetland Park

MAP C2 ■ Tin Shui Wai, New Territories ■ 3152 2666 ■ Open 10am–5pm Wed–Mon ■ Adm ■ www.wetlandpark.gov.hk

This landscaped wetlands area on the border with China has bird hides, a butterfly garden, lily ponds and a mangrove circuit featuring mud-skippers and fiddler crabs. There is also a great, informative walk-through environmental display.

🔟 Nightclubs

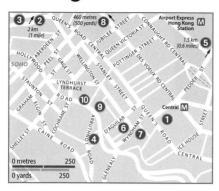

1 Faye
MAP K5 ■ 25–26th Floor, California Tower, D'Aguilar St ■ 3619 4282

Perched on the top of California Tower, Faye overlooks Hong Kong's bustling Central district, home to some of the city's most enviable bars and restaurants. Have dinner in the neighbourhood then head for a couple of drinks at Faye, partying into the night. Do prize yourself away from the dance floor at some point – the rooftop views are excellent.

2 Ozone at the Ritz-Carlton
MAP L2 ■ Ritz-Carlton Hong Kong, 1 Austin Rd W ■ 2263 2270

Taking the honours as one of the highest bars in the world, Ozone sits on floor 118 of the Ritz-Carlton, with outdoor seating and impressive Victoria Harbour views.

3 FLM
MAP K5 ■ 62 Jervois St, Sheung Wan ■ 2799 2883 ■ www.flmhk.net

One of Hong Kong's long-standing icons, FLM has kept the party going well into the night, through many years and changed names. Conveniently located right across other LGBTQ+ bars such as Wink and Zoo, this bar attracts a varied crowd. Definitely one of the bars in the city that cannot be missed. It gets busy on weekends.

4 Dragon-i
Two completely different rooms are meticulously-designed – merging Chinese, Japanese and American aesthetics. The Red Room dining room becomes a VIP lounge for the famous as the evening progresses, with everyone else sinking into the booths in the bronze and mirrored "Playground", drinking powerful cocktails. The Dragon-i (see p70) is a nightspot for the stylish set, so you'll need to dress accordingly.

Stylish interior at Ozone at the Ritz-Carlton

Sophisticated setting at The Cocktail Bar at Felix Restaurant

5 The Cocktail Bar at Felix Restaurant

Set in Kowloon's famous Peninsula Hotel, this shinning pinancle of Hong Kong bars *(see p91)* has been designed by Philippe Starck. From the dedicated elevators with their light effects, to the elegantly-designed restrooms, the entire experience envelops you. The harbour views are an added bonus. If you plan to visit just one bar in Hong Kong, make this the one.

6 Rula Live

A well-known Irish bar in Lan Kwai Fong, Rula Live *(see p70)* was relaunched in 2019. Featuring live music, this Hong Kong institution has a trendy urban warehouse feel, with exposed steal beams and walls. Sip inventive cocktails or the many craft beers on offer while enjoying the dance that follows the band performances.

7 Play

MAP K5 ■ 1 On Hing Terrace, Central ■ www.playclub.asia

Hong Kong's largest single-floor nightclub, Play is split into three distinctive rooms, including two main rooms and a champagne bar. Top DJs and finest cocktail mixologists keep the trendy club clientele partying into the early hours of the morning.

8 (Mihn) Club

MAP J4 ■ 4th floor, 279 Des Voeux Rd Central, Sheung Wan ■ 5818 3870

Named after the Chinese character "radical" that suggests a roof or a shelter, this club makes everyone feel at home. Electronic music lovers can expect banging playlists at the 100-capacity venue. Guest DJs keep things fresh, with the club known for hosting the best up-and-coming acts in Hong Kong and beyond.

9 Di Vino

MAP K5 ■ 73 Wyndham St, Central ■ 2167 8883 ■ www.divino group.com

This tunnel-shaped wine bar and restaurant offers a perfect start to any evening. It has special prices on early-evening aperitifs and a wide range of wines available by the glass. There are also bar snacks and sharing plates.

10 OMA

MAP K5 ■ 79 Wyndham St, Central ■ 2521 8815

This excellent underground music venue has an intimate and friendly setting. OMA treats its patrons to live band performances before midnight, followed by some of the best house, techno and trance music you'll hear in the city. A good time is guaranteed.

🔟 Hong Kong Dishes

A plate of *cha siu*

1 Cha Siu
This is virtually Hong Kong's national dish. The name literally means "fork roast". The tender fillets of pork are roasted and glazed in honey and spices, and hung in the windows of specialist roast meat shops. *Cha siu* is classically served thinly sliced, with steamed rice and strips of vegetables.

Traditional moon cake

2 Moon Cake
Made of moist pastry and various fillings, including lotus, taro, *azuki* bean, whole egg yolk and occasionally coconut, the delicacy also has a quirky history: revolutionaries in imperial China used to smuggle messages to each other hidden in the cake's dense filling.

3 Steamed Whole Fish
In Hong Kong, fish is almost always dressed very simply, using only peanut oil, soya sauce, chives and coriander. To maximize freshness, restaurants keep tanks of live fish, which are prepared to order.

4 French Toast
Slathered with butter, fried, and served with syrup, Hong Kong's twist on French toast is far from the healthiest thing on the menu, but that's besides the point. This sweet and savoury staple is quintessential Hong Kong local food, and can be found at the majority of local cafés.

5 Brisket of Beef
Requiring up to 8 hours of slow cooking, preparation of this Hong Kong classic is an art. Households and restaurants guard their individual recipes, but all involve the classic five Chinese spices, rock sugar and tangerine peel. It's served in an earthenware pot as a main course, or as a topping for rice or noodles. Given the dish's richness, it is particularly enjoyed during the cooler winter months.

6 Wontons
Prepared traditionally, these marvellous prawn and pork Chinese ravioli are poached in a stock made from shrimp roe, aniseed and other spices, and served with fresh egg noodles and soup.

7 Water Spinach
The leafy, hollow-stemmed vegetable can be prepared with various seasonings, from the quotidian oyster sauce to garlic and shrimp paste. At its best when stir-fried with potent chillies and semi-fermented tofu.

Fried water spinach with chilli

8 Fish Balls

A daily food for many Hong Kongers, either on skewers as snacks or served with noodles in broth to make a meal. Traditional restaurants eschew machine production methods, and still shape these balls of minced fish, white pepper and other spices by hand, before poaching them in seafood or chicken stock.

Fish balls in curry sauce

9 Salt and Pepper Crusted Squid

This dish is far removed from the fried squid you'll find in Western Chinatowns. Banish that memory from your mind, and prepare to discover the gloriously crisp original. Fresh squid is scored, lightly battered and flash fried with lots of salt, white pepper, chilli and garlic. The result is an addictive combination of tangy textures.

10 Nai Wong Bau

Chinese bread is shaped into buns, not loaves, and steamed rather than baked – giving it a beautifully soft and fluffy quality (no gritty whole grains here). There are many varieties of Chinese sweet bun, but *nai wong bau* is the reigning favourite, the kind of treat that children will clamour for. These buns are filled with a mixture of milk, eggs, coconut and sugar. Try them piping hot on a cold winter morning.

TOP 10 DIM SUM (DUMPLINGS)

Dim sum in steaming baskets

1 Har Gow
Prawns wrapped in a rice-flour casing and then steamed – like a very plump, transparent ravioli.

2 Siu Mai
Traditional minced pork and shrimp parcels, topped with a dab of crab roe or diced carrot.

3 Seen Juk Guen
Soy pastry, crisp fried with a vegetable filling. A savvy alternative to the common spring roll.

4 Gai Zaht
Chicken and ham wrapped in soyabean sheets, served in rich sauce.

5 Lor Bak Go
Shredded Chinese radish, pan-fried with chives, dried shrimp and Chinese salami, then steamed to form a "cake".

6 Cheung Fun
Rolls of rice pastry, filled with shrimp, pork or beef, and smothered in sweet soy sauce.

7 Chiu Chow Fun Gor
Soft dumplings filled with chopped nuts, minced pork and pickled vegetables inside a thin layer of dough.

8 Jin Yeung Lat Jiu
Green pepper stuffed with minced fish and prawns and served in a classic black-bean sauce.

9 Ji Ma Wu
Decadent, treacle-like dessert made from sugar and mashed sesame. It is served warm from the trolley.

10 Ma Lai Goh
Wonderfully light and fluffy steamed sponge cake, made with eggs, brown sugar and walnuts.

🔟 Restaurants

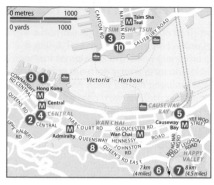

classic French culinary traditions with distinctive Asian influences without ever becoming "fusion". This restaurant is simply outstanding, as its three Michelin stars imply, and is popular for meat and seafood dishes.

1 Caprice

A two Michelin-starred restaurant (see p71) with views of the harbour, this is fine French dining at its most sumptuous; expect outstanding cuisine, excellent Bordeaux and Burgundy wines and lavish decor. Set-menu lunches draw a strong business crowd, while evenings and weekend lunches are definitely "see and be seen" affairs.

Fine decor at Caprice

2 L'Atelier de Joël Robuchon

L'Atelier (see p71) is a highly contemporary venue decorated in bright scarlet with high-top seats arranged around an open kitchen. The set menu options combine

3 T'ang Court

The food at T'ang Court, Langham Hotel's three Michelin-starred restaurant (see p91), continues to astonish. Peerless creativity and insistence on *wok chi* (wok cooking at the highest achievable temperature) are its top qualities. The restaurant is spread over two floors – upstairs is quieter while the lower floor is open plan.

4 8½ Otto e Mezzo Bombana

This superb contemporary Italian restaurant (see p71) was upgraded from two to three Michelin stars in 2011, the first Italian restaurant outside Italy to achieve that recognition. Chef Umberto Bombana, dubbed "The King of White Truffles", weaves his culinary magic using only the freshest ingredients. The name is taken from Italian director Federico Fellini's 1963 Oscar-winning autobiographical film.

5 Kung Tak Lam

Though common, meat isn't necessarily a staple in Chinese food. Veggie-friendly dim sum is the specialty at Kung Tak Lam (see p77) – the go-to spot for vegetarians in the city. This airy Shanghainese does things with vegetables that could not even be imagined by most vegetarian restaurants elsewhere. There is another branch in Tsim Sha Tsui, but this 10th-floor location can't be beaten for its excellent harbour views.

The Verandah's elegant interior

8 Peking Garden

With interiors decorated in sumptuous traditional style, this centrally located restaurant *(see p71)* has served high-end Chinese cuisine for decades. Classic Peking duck, which never fails to impress, is the most sought-after dish here. Other signature dishes include deep-fried prawns in chilli sauce as well as deep-fried fish with sweet and sour sauce and pine nuts.

9 Lung King Heen

The world's first Chinese to earn three Michelin stars is a beautifully styled modern Cantonese restaurant *(see p71)*. Lung King Heen means "View of the Dragon" and the interior is designed to replicate a Chinese landscape. It is particularly strong on seafood dishes and dim sum, which can be enjoyed while taking in the splendid harbour views.

6 The Verandah

From its epic Sunday brunches through to romantic, candle-lit dinners, this Southside patrician *(see p83)* offers impeccable service and enjoys a well-deserved lead over nearby competition. The elegant interior has lovely views through shuttered windows over treetops and of the sea. Go for the fresh oysters and the Grand Marnier soufflé.

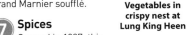

Vegetables in crispy nest at Lung King Heen

7 Spices

Opened in 1987, this popular restaurant *(see p83)* is set in a colonial-style building, with bamboo and teak elements, attached to The Repulse Bay hotel. Sip on cocktails and dine on classic Asian cuisine at a table in the landscaped garden, which overlooks the bay.

10 Gaddi's

Royalty, Hollywood stars and heads of state have all been known to dine here. In terms of French cuisine in the city, Gaddi's *(see p91)* is the holy grail. Expect the highest level in every area: from the sophisticated menu to ultra-attentive service. If you are a fan of *haute cuisine*, you've found your culinary heaven.

Opulent dining room at Gaddi's

🔟 Markets

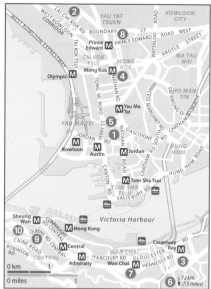

coterie of fortune tellers and perhaps even a Chinese Opera recital.

2 Apliu Street Flea Market

The flea market (see p102) at Sham Shui Po is a treasure trove of second-hand household goods and utter junk, strewn either side of the pavement in makeshift stalls. It's the most fun of Hong Kong's street markets, not least because you just might uncover one of the genuine vintage collectables that occasionally surfaces here. It's also a good place to pick up pre-loved mobile phones and electronic gadgetry.

1 Temple Street Night Market

This bustling, atmospheric market (see pp22–3) comes alive at night. Hundreds of stalls are jam-packed by 9pm, offering pirated goods and all manner of junk. It used to be known as Men's Street, and many stalls still stock less-than-fashionable attire. Venture past the market and you'll stumble onto a lamplit

3 Jardine's Bazaar and Jardine's Crescent

MAP Q6 ■ Jardine's Bazaar, Causeway Bay, Hong Kong Island ■ Open 11am–9:30pm daily

An open-air market area in the heart of Causeway Bay, one of Hong Kong's busiest shopping districts. All sorts of goodies are available here, from run-of-the-mill fashion shops to traditional barbers and Chinese medicine sellers. Try some fresh soy bean milk.

Market trader selling masks at Temple Street Night Market

Shoppers at Ladies' Market

8 Flower Market
MAP E4 ■ Flower Market Rd, Prince Edward ■ Open 9:30am–7:30pm daily

Breath in the scent from dozens of little flower shops *(see p93)*. Many of them sell not just roses and tulips, but orchids and tropical blooms too, along with subtle arrangements and auspicious houseplants.

9 Graham Street
MAP K5

It's a shock to find Graham Street's crush of down-to-earth market stalls just a stone's throw from Central's sophisticated boutiques. You might want to avoid the confrontational butcher's shops, but it's worth a visit to see how ordinary Hong Kongers buy their groceries.

4 Ladies' Market
No designer labels – unless they're fake. What you'll find at Ladies' Market *(see p95)* is inexpensive women's clothing from lingerie to shoes. There's a decent selection of jeans, plus cheap food and trinkets galore.

5 Jade Market
As you might suppose, jade sellers abound – more than 450 of them at the last count. Don't attempt to buy the top-grade stuff unless you're an expert and know what you are doing. But there are plenty of cheaper pieces to be found here *(see p94)*.

Pendant, Jade Market

10 Cat Street
MAP J5 ■ Upper Lascar Row, Sheung Wan ■ Open 11am–5pm daily

The name refers to the Chinese slang for "odds and ends". The market here and on nearby Hollywood Road are chock-full of antique and curio shops. This is the place to come for silk carpets, elegant Chinese furniture, Ming dynasty ceramic horsemen and Maoist kitsch.

6 Stanley Market
Particularly frenetic at the weekend, this traditional open-air market *(see pp20–21)* is perpetually teeming with visitors who come here to shop for bric-a-brac, souvenirs, casual clothes and home decor. If you're not claustrophobic, head to the narrow lanes to hunt for bargains.

7 Tai Yuen Street Toy Market
MAP N6 ■ Wan Chai ■ Open 11am–7pm daily

The stalls here sell the latest trendy items and traditional Chinese and Western toys, as well as pieces from Hong Kong's pre-1980s past when it was a centre of toy manufacturing.

Traditional dolls on Cat Street

🔟 Hong Kong for Free

Nan Lian Garden, Kowloon

1 Gardens

Hong Kong's peaceful and stunning gardens are a dream for nature lovers. The Nan Lian Garden, opposite Chi Lin Nunnery *(see p102)* in Diamond Hill, is a Tang Dynasty-style landscape garden with a *koi* pond and a traditional tea house. Minutes away from the busy Central district is the Zoological and Botanical Gardens, a showcase of the city's flora and fauna.

2 Harbour Views

Admire Hong Kong's busy harbour and dynamic architecture from a number of free viewpoints: The Peak offers the most impressive panoramas; Central Plaza's 46th-floor Sky Lobby in Wan Chai, though not a formal viewing platform, offers great views; or watch the evening light show from the Tsim Sha Tsui waterfront.

3 Mid-Levels Escalator

For an effortless, free ride uphill through the busy market and entertainment district, catch the unique Mid-Levels Escalator between Central and SoHo *(see p67)*.

You are rewarded with great views of historic architecture and vignettes of street life in the lanes below. Get off to shop for trinkets along the way on Hollywood Road.

4 Beaches

They may not be the first to come to mind when you think of Hong Kong, but beautiful beaches are found in the city. For the clearest waters and the softest sand, head to Sai Kung *(see p110)*. The sun-soaked peninsula is dotted with pristine beaches – rest assured they'll make the trek to get there worthwhile.

5 Country Parks
MAP C2–E5

Take a break from the concrete jungle and wander into Hong Kong's backyard. The city has 24 country parks, each with their own gems. Aberdeen Country Park in the south has an expansive reservoir. Don't miss the Tai Tong stretch of Tai Lam Country Park in November or December, when the leaves on the gum trees turn yellow, orange and red.

6 Martial Arts

Martial arts are an integral element of Hong Kong's culture but, despite what you'll see in the movies, the real thing often tends to be hidden away from public view. You can strike lucky in the nearest park at dawn, or catch the free 2-hour shows held at Kowloon Park's Kung Fu Corner *(see p87)* every Sunday afternoon.

Martial artists in Kowloon Park

7 Hiking

Hong Kong is covered in hiking trails; some of them are surprisingly tough and all wind through large swathes of the territory that have so far escaped development. Hong Kong Island's Dragon's Back trail offers an accessible, relatively easy introduction, and ends with a beach and supper at Shek O (see p80).

8 Temples

Hong Kong's many temples are free to visit (although change for the collection box is appreciated). Try the Man Mo Temple on Hollywood Road (see p67), the Tin Hau Temple off Nathan Road in Yau Ma Tei (see p74) or the Wong Tai Sin Temple in eastern Kowloon (see p101).

Camping on Ham Tin Wan beach

9 Camping

 www.afcd.gov.hk

Surprisingly, for a city where even cramped, budget accommodation usually comes at a premium, there are 41 free campsites spread across Hong Kong's New Territories, and some of them are in spectacular settings. The downsides are that they operate on a first-come-first-served basis, are all fairly remote and have only basic facilities.

10 Cultural Events

Head out to the foyer of the Hong Kong Cultural Centre (see p86) for free performances which mostly take place on Saturday afternoons and occasional weekday lunchtimes. The Fringe Club (see p70) hosts free exhibitions and events. There are also various free events in the area around the Hong Kong Observation Wheel on the waterfront (see p66).

TOP 10 BUDGET TIPS

Food stalls at a produce market

1 Food Stalls
For the cheapest meals, eat at the food stalls at the indoor produce markets.

2 Museum Wednesdays
Most of Hong Kong's museums offer free admission on Wednesdays.

3 Happy Valley Racecourse
At only HK$10 for entry, Happy Valley Racecourse (see pp16–17) offers a cheap night out.

4 Chungking Mansions
Find the best deals on budget accommodation, including clean and comfortable guesthouses and basic hostels at Chungking Mansions (see p87).

5 Star Ferry
The cheapest way to cross Hong Kong harbour is aboard the Star Ferry (see pp18–19), which has stunning views.

6 Octopus Card
Save time and money on Hong Kong's public transport system with an Octopus Card (see p140).

7 Happy Hour
Many of Hong Kong's bars and clubs offer relatively inexpensive drinks during daily happy hours.

8 Hotel Shuttles
A free shuttle service runs from the Airport Express stations in Kowloon and Central to and from local hotels.

9 Shenzhen Airport
Shenzhen airport offers cheaper flights into China than those from Hong Kong.

10 Markets and Malls
For the best prices on electronics, clothes, antiques and souvenirs, check out dedicated markets and malls.

🔟 Festivals and Events

① Chinese New Year
Three days from the first day of the first moon, usually late Jan/early Feb

Hong Kong's most celebrated festival is a riot of neon and noise. Skyscrapers on both sides of the harbour are lit up to varying degrees, depending on the vicissitudes of the economy; fireworks explode over the harbour, shops shut and residents give doormen *lai see* (lucky money) as they exchange festive greetings.

② Spring Lantern Festival (Yuen Siu)
The 15th day of the lunar calendar (end Feb)

Also known as Hong Kong's Valentine's Day, this festival marks the end of the traditional Chinese New Year celebrations. Beautiful glowing lanterns are hung in parks and flower markets, and couples stroll hand in hand.

③ Art Basel Hong Kong
Mar (dates vary) ■ **www. artbasel.com**

A significant festival for the city's contemporary art community, Art Basel sees galleries from all over Asia and the Asia-Pacific come together. Highly regarded, it gives up-and-coming and established artists a pivotal platform from which to showcase their work.

Dragon boat race at Stanley Beach

④ Ching Ming
First week of Apr

Also known as the grave-sweeping festival, *ching ming* means "clear and bright". This is when Chinese families visit the graves of their ancestors to clear them of any weeds and wilted flowers. Many people also light incense and burn paper money.

⑤ Tin Hau Festival
The 23rd day of the 3rd moon (Apr/May)

This is the big one if you make your living from the sea. Fishermen make floral paper offerings to Tin Hau, the goddess of the sea, hoping for fine weather and full nets. The best celebrations are held at the temples at Stanley, Joss House Bay or Tin Hau Temple Road.

⑥ Cheung Chau Bun Festival
MAP C6 ■ **The 6th day of the 4th moon (Apr/May), Cheung Chau**

For four days, the island disappears under clouds of incense smoke and exuberant crowds. Highlights include a parade of children in period costumes, and a thrilling midnight race to scale 8-m- (26-ft-) high towers made of buns.

⑦ Dragon Boat Festival (Tuen Ng)
The 5th day of the 5th moon (May/ early Jun); various locations

Drums thunder and paddles churn the waters of Hong Kong as garish

craft vie for the top prize. The festival honours Qu Yuan, a 3rd-century poet-statesman who drowned himself to protest against corrupt rulers.

⑧ Hungry Ghost Festival (Yue Laan)
Jul, various locations
From the 14th day of the seventh moon, the Chinese believe the gates of hell are thrown open and the undead run riot on earth for a month. Lots more "hell money" goes up in smoke, as do various hillsides. This is not a good time for hiking.

Lanterns, Mid-Autumn Festival

⑨ Mid-Autumn Festival
The 15th night of the 8th moon (Aug)
Celebrated since the time of the early Tang Dynasty in the 7th century, this festival features colourful lantern displays, the mass consumption of moon cakes and a Fire-dragon Dance in Tai Hang district, where a long dragon is run through the lanes at night. The best carnival is held in Victoria Park.

⑩ Hong Kong Pride
Nov ▪ www.hkpride.net
In a relatively conservative society, the city's Pride Parade is a modest but growing event that has gained support over the years. The parade usually starts in Victoria Park.

TOP 10 SPORTING EVENTS

Macau Grand Prix

1 Standard Chartered Hong Kong Marathon
Jan/Feb ▪ 2577 0800 ▪ www.hk marathon.com
The gruelling race covers the entire city.

2 Lunar New Year Cup
Feb ▪ Hong Kong Stadium ▪ www.hkfa.com
A Hong Kong football team battles it out with international competition.

3 Rugby Sevens
Mar/Apr ▪ www.hksevens.com
Fast rugby and beer-fuelled mayhem.

4 International Dragon Boat Races
May/Jun ▪ Sha Tin
Festive boats compete on the Shing Mun River and other locations, including Victoria Harbour.

5 Cricket Sixes
Oct ▪ Kowloon Cricket Club ▪ www.hkcricket.org
Top players take part in action around the stumps. Check the website to ensure the event is going ahead.

6 New World Harbour Race
Oct ▪ 2572 8594 ▪ www.hkharbourrace.com
Adrenaline junkies take to Hong Kong's harbour for a competitive swim.

7 HK Badminton Open
Nov ▪ Hong Kong Coliseum ▪ 2504 8318 ▪ www.hkopenbadminton.org
International badminton stars.

8 Oxfam Trailwalker
Nov ▪ 2520 2525 ▪ www.oxfam trailwalker.org.hk
A gruelling walk over MacLehose Trail.

9 Macau Grand Prix
Nov ▪ www.macau.grandprix.gov.mo
Formula 3 action in the former Portuguese enclave.

10 Hong Kong Open
Nov/Dec ▪ www.ubshkopen.com
Prestigious annual golf tournament.

Hong Kong
Area by Area

Central's skyline as seen
from Victoria Peak

TOP 10 Hong Kong Island – Northwest

Water Buffalo by Elisabeth Frink, Exchange Square

From the architectural wonders of Central district's glass towers, through the vodka bars and galleries of SoHo, and spilling down flagstone lanes to the raucous shophouses and old docksides of Western, the Island's northwest potently concentrates all of Hong Kong's surreal contradictions. In the concrete gullies between futuristic banks and statement office blocks you'll find traditional street markets, temples and herbalists, all carrying on like some Hollywood dream of old Chinatown. These are some of the most mercantile streets in human history. A shot of snake-bile wine, or a fierce macchiato? In this part of the city, you can have it all.

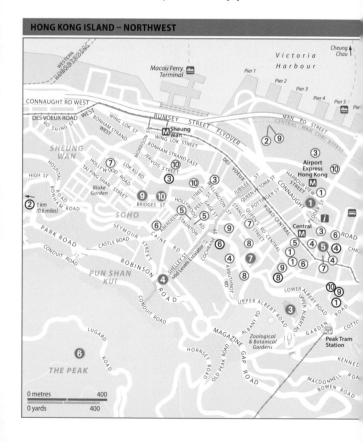

HONG KONG ISLAND – NORTHWEST

1 Exchange Square
MAP L5

As the name suggests, Exchange Square is home to Hong Kong's red-carpeted financial engine room, although the stock exchange is not open to visitors. However, the peaceful square outside it, dominated by a large fountain, is a great place to picnic. Near the fountain are sculptures by Henry Moore and Dame Elisabeth Frink. The square's tallest building, Two IFC Tower *(see pp38–9)*, was designed by Cesar Pelli.

2 Hong Kong Park
MAP L6

This park's open spaces and mature trees make an excellent escape, particularly the strikingly elegant

Hong Kong Park and aviary

(and free) walk-through aviary. The flowing streams and lush plant life of this improbable mini-rainforest are a peaceful and shaded home to scores of bird species. The park also has lakes, a large conservatory, a viewing tower and the free Museum of Teaware, inside Flagstaff House.

3 Former Government House
MAP L6

This grand old building served as the British governor's residence from 1855 until 1997, when the last governor, Chris Patten, handed Hong Kong back to China. Patten's successor, Tung Chee-hwa, cited bad feng shui created by the needle-like Bank of China Tower *(see p38)* as one reason not to move in, opting to remain in his house on The Peak. Back in the 1940s, the occupying Japanese added the Shinto-style towers to the Georgian structure, which at one time enjoyed harbour views. It is used for official functions, and only open occasionally to the public – contact HKTB *(see p145)*.

4 The Escalator
MAP K5

A wonderful feature of Hong Kong is its 792-m- (2,598-ft-) long string of escalators, which links all the roads between Queen's Road and Conduit Street. It's the best way for pedestrians to get around the steep districts of Central, the Mid-Levels and SoHo. The Escalator runs uphill until midnight, except during the morning rush hour, when it runs downhill.

5 Central's Statue Square

Arguably the heart and soul of Hong Kong, Statue Square (see pp14–15) is home to some of the city's most iconic buildings. These include the angular Bank of China building, two of Hong Kong's most famous shopping malls, as well as the Neo-Classical Court of Appeal and the red-brick Former French Mission which serve as reminders of this region's colonial history. Also located here is the Chater Garden, which is an oasis of peace amid the city's usual bustle.

6 The Peak

Towering over Hong Kong Central and dwarfing even its highest buildings, The Peak (see pp12–13) is a much-loved urban retreat, offering an escape from the city's heat during summer. With its plethora of affluent neighbourhoods home to billionaires and celebrities, the area has become almost synonymous with luxury. Take the funicular tram up to admire the breathtaking views, indulge in some shopping and grab a bite to eat.

7 Lan Kwai Fong

MAP K5

Lan Kwai Fong (or Orchid Square) only really starts to buzz at night when office workers, including plenty of city suits, come here to unwind at

PLAGUE

In the 19th century, Hong Kong, just like many other parts of the world in history, suffered devastating plagues incubated in filthy, crowded slums. It was also in Hong Kong where, in 1894, the source of the plague was identified, almost simultaneously, by two doctors. The discovery of the bacteria went on to revolutionize the prevention and treatment of plague.

its many restaurants, bars and clubs. The street is packed with revellers on Fridays. The partying spills across to tiny Wing Wah Lane, just opposite D'Aguilar Street, which houses bars and a decent selection of good-value Thai, Malay and Indian restaurants.

8 The Waterfront

MAP L–M5 ■ Hong Kong Observation Wheel: open noon–9pm Mon–Thu, 11am–11pm Fri–Sun; adm; www.hkow.hk

Turn right out of the Central Star Ferry for some open waterside space and benches with good views across to Kowloon. To the east is the imposing Hong Kong Observation Wheel, a Ferris wheel overlooking the harbour. The waterfront hosts A Symphony of Lights (see p19), the laser-and-sound show that lights up the buildings around the harbour every evening.

The Waterfront, seen from across the harbour in Kowloon

The altar at Man Mo Temple

⑨ Man Mo Temple
MAP J5 ▪ Western end, Hollywood Rd

The sombre red-and-gold interior of Man Mo Temple, dating back to the 1840s, is always thick with sandalwood smoke from the giant incense spirals hanging overhead, which take a couple of weeks to burn through. The temple is dedicated to two deities, Man (the god of literature) and Mo (the god of war). Some of the scenes from the 1960 film version of Richard Mason's *The World of Suzie Wong* were filmed here.

⑩ Hollywood Road
MAP J–K5

This mecca for Chinese antiques and curios may no longer offer the bargains it once did, but Hollywood Road's eastern end is still jammed with kitschy antiques shops. The shops on Upper Lascar Row are relatively cheaper. South of this road lies the buzzing SoHo area, with stylish bars, cafés, restaurants, as well as upscale boutiques and art galleries dotted all around Elgin, Staunton and Shelley streets.

Buddha figure, Hollywood Road

A DAY IN CENTRAL

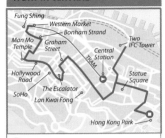

▶ MORNING

From Des Voeux Road take the tram westwards from Central and get off outside the handsome colonial building housing **Western Market** at 323 Des Voeux Road. Browse among the ground-floor trinkets or select a pattern from the many bolts of material on the first floor. The nearby **Fung Shing** restaurant *(21 Connaught Rd W)* serves excellent dim sum.

The streets around nearby Bonham Strand contain dried-seafood shops, Chinese apothecaries, and paper offering shops. Head uphill to the atmospheric **Man Mo Temple**, then east past the antique shops of **Hollywood Road**, browsing stalls as you go.

Break for lunch or a drink in one of the many restaurants and bars on the streets to the south of **SoHo** or below **Hollywood Road** in Lan Kwai Fong.

AFTERNOON

Check out fresh produce market stalls around the **Escalator** *(see p65)* and **Graham Street** *(see p57)* before hitting the colonial heart of Hong Kong Island, **Statue Square**.

Choose to visit the **upmarket malls** *(see p69)*, or for some peace and harbour views head to Queen's Pier. For altitude and a spectacular city perspective go up to the HKMA Information Centre on the 55th floor of **Two IFC Tower** *(see p38–9)*.

Quiet and shade are found in the nearby **Hong Kong Park** *(see p65)*.

See map on pp64–5 ←

Historical Relics

Nave of St John's Cathedral

1 St John's Cathedral
MAP L6 ■ 4–8 Garden Rd

Resembling a parish church more than a cathedral, St John's, completed in 1849, is the oldest Anglican church in east Asia.

2 University of Hong Kong
MAP F3 ■ Pok Fu Lam ■ www.hku.hk

This institution is home to many "declared monuments" – historic sites that must be preserved. Check out Main Building, Eliot Hall and May Hall.

3 Old Letter Box
MAP L5

A few traditional green, cast-iron post boxes bearing the British royal cipher remain. There is one at the northern end of Statue Square.

19th-century post box

4 Colonial Street Names
MAP K5–6

Most colonial buildings have been sacrificed to new development, but the legacy is preserved in many of the roads named after royals (Queen's Road), politicians (Peel Street), military officers (D'Aguilar, Pedder) and public servants (Bonham, Des Voeux).

5 Former Military Hospital
MAP L6 ■ Bowen Rd

Broken into separate units – some abandoned – the huge, grand old building, built from 1903 to 1906 between Bowen and Borrett roads, used to serve as a military hospital.

6 Hollywood Road Police Station
MAP K5

Bastions of colonial law and order, the Police Station (1864) and the old Victoria Prison (1841) still stand.

7 Flagstaff House
MAP L6 ■ Hong Kong Park

Built in the mid-1840s, Flagstaff House is one of the oldest colonial buildings on the island and houses the free Museum of Teaware.

8 Duddell Street
MAP K5 ■ Off Ice House St

While not spectacular, the gas lamps and old steps of Duddell Street date back to the 1920s and 1870s respectively.

9 Court of Final Appeal
MAP L5

The elegant 1911 Neo-Classical building served as the city's Supreme Court and then as its Legislative HQ until the Court of Final Appeal relocated here in 2015.

10 Former French Mission
MAP L6 ■ Battery Path

This red-brick building was built in 1843 as the home of the first governor of Hong Kong. Restyled as the French Mission HQ in 1917, it later housed the Court of Final Appeal.

The handsome Former French Mission

Upmarket Malls and Boutiques

Spacious lobby and luxury boutiques at The Landmark

1 The Landmark
MAP L5 ■ Pedder St

A modern mall with conspicuous consumables from the likes of Chanel, Dior, Armani, Paul Smith, Prada, Vuitton, Bulgari and Tiffany.

2 Harvey Nichols
MAP M6 ■ Pacific Place, 88 Queensway, Admiralty or 15 Queen's Rd, Central

Designer clothes, cosmetics, and food at the two Hong Kong branches of the luxury British department store.

3 Lane Crawford
MAP L4 ■ IFC Mall, 8 Finance St

Upmarket clothing, with concessions from most big Western designer brands, house-ware, beauty products, glass and porcelain, and Asia's largest women's shoe shop.

4 Landmark Prince's
MAP L5 ■ Ice House St or Des Voeux Rd Central

The bright, airy and less crowded Prince's Building is worth a visit if you would like to peruse big-name clothes and accessory designers.

5 G.O.D.
MAP K5 ■ 48 Hollywood Rd, Central

The Goods of Desire (G.O.D.) is an ultra-hip store that offers an off-beat selection of Chinese-inspired furnishings, accessories as well as clothing.

6 Gucci
MAP L5 ■ The Landmark, G1

This beautiful temple to the brand of Gucci is its lavish Hong Kong flag-ship. While away the hours window shopping the divine clothes and beautiful accessories.

7 Dragon Culture
MAP K5 ■ 231 Hollywood Rd

An antiques shop, Dragon Culture features pottery from most dynasties, bamboo carvings, jades and plenty more.

8 Lock Cha Tea Shop
MAP L6 ■ G/F K.S.Lo Gallery, Hong Kong Park, Admiralty

Around 100 varieties of tea, along with traditional and modern teaware, is sold by experts in a colonial-era building. Try the tasty dim sum.

9 Shanghai Tang
MAP K–L5 ■ 1 Duddell St, Central

Local entrepreneur David Tang is behind this international brand, which takes a smart twist on traditional Chinese clothes and ornaments. Jackets and kitsch Mao watches are staples.

10 Two IFC
MAP L5 ■ 8 Finance St, Central

Hong Kong's smartest mall features a selection of top brands, including an Apple Store. There is also a superb supermarket and a cinema.

See map on pp64–5

Bars and Clubs

The smart interior of MO Bar at the Mandarin Oriental

1 MO Bar
MAP L5 ▪ The Landmark
Mandarin Oriental, 15 Queen's Rd,
Central ▪ 2132 0077
The glamorous bar at the legendary
Mandarin Oriental is the place to go
for cocktails, and all-day dining. It
is also a sophisticated night spot.

2 Café Gray Deluxe
MAP M6 ▪ 49/F The Upper
House Hotel, Pacific Place, 88
Queensway ▪ 3968 1106
This swanky cocktail and wine
lounge at the swish Upper House
Hotel has superb harbour views.

3 COA
MAP K5 ▪ Shop A, LG/F
Wah Shin House, 6–10 Shin Hing St,
Central ▪ 2813 5787
Renowned as one of Asia's best bars,
COA's artisanal cocktails feature the
very best of agave spirits.

4 Dragon-i
MAP K5 ▪ UG/F The Centrium,
60 Wyndham St ▪ 3110 1222
The most happening club (see p50) in
Central, where models, movers and
shakers and celebrities from Jackie
Chan to Sting have been spotted.

5 The Globe
MAP K5 ▪ 45–53A Graham St,
Central ▪ 2543 1941
Hong Kong's best beer bar serves
locally micro-brewed beers and rare
tap beers from around the world.

6 The Old Man
MAP K5 ▪ Lower G/F, 37–39
Aberdeen St, Soho, Central ▪ 2703 1899
This Ernest Hemingway-inspired bar
is a cocktail haven. Watch bartenders
work their magic with the classics or
try something original.

7 Sevva
MAP L5 ▪ 25/F Prince's Bldg,
10 Chater Rd, Central ▪ 2537 1388
Bonnie Gokson's beautifully designed
bar and restaurant is among the
city's most stylish hangouts.

8 Rúla Live
MAP K5 ▪ G/F, 58–62
D'Aguilar St, Lan Kwai Fong,
Central ▪ 6031 2116
A long-standing favourite of locals,
Rúla Live (see p51) features live
music followed by DJs and excellent
cocktails and craft beers.

9 Tell Camellia
MAP K5 ▪ LG Floor, H Code,
45 Pottinger St, Central ▪ 9821 5501
A must-visit for tea lovers, Tell
Camellia's bartenders fuse tea and
cocktail culture. Try the Oolong old-
fashioned or the Darjeeling negroni.

10 Zoo Bar
MAP K5 ▪ 33 Jervois St,
Sheung Wan ▪ 3583 1200
Pioneering the popularity of this
area, the Zoo Bar, a favourite of the
LGBTQ+ community, is a natural pit
stop for anyone after a good time.

Restaurants

 Lei Garden
MAP K5 ▪ Shop 3008,
3/F IFC Mall ▪ 2295 0238 ▪ $$$

This multi-award-winning chain-restaurant serves modern Cantonese food as it should be – light, delicate and subtle.

 Lung King Heen
MAP L4 ▪ Four Seasons Hotel, 8 Finance St, Central ▪ 3196 8880 ▪ $$$

Executive chef Chan Yan Tak is the mastermind behind this contemporary Cantonese restaurant (see p55), which has earned three Michelin stars.

Lung King Heen dining room

 Peking Garden
MAP L5 ▪ B1 Alexandra House, 16–20 Chater Rd, Central ▪ 2526 6456 ▪ $$$

A popular spot among locals, Peking Garden (see p55) offers excellent thinly-sliced Beijing duck.

8½ Otto e Mezzo Bombana
MAP L5 ▪ 202 Landmark Alexandra, 18 Chater Rd, Central ▪ 2537 8859 ▪ Closed Sun ▪ $$$

This three Michelin-starred place (see p54) serves excellent Italian fare.

L'Atelier de Joël Robuchon
MAP L5 ▪ 401 The Landmark ▪ 2166 9000 ▪ $$$

Superstar chef Joël Robuchon picks up Michelin stars almost wherever

PRICE CATEGORIES
For a three-course meal for one with half a bottle of wine and extra charges. Prices are quoted in Hong Kong dollars.

$ under $250 $$ $250–600 $$$ over $600

he sets up a restaurant (see p54). Expect perfectly executed French classics with a hint of Asian flair.

 The Mandarin Grill & Bar
MAP L5 ▪ Mandarin Oriental, 5 Connaught Rd ▪ 2825 4004 ▪ $$$

The interior may have been revamped by Sir Terence Conran, but the menu still features English classics and premium seafood. It's held its Michelin star since 2009.

 Yat Lok Roast Goose
MAP K5 ▪ 34–38 Stanley St, Central ▪ 2524 3882 ▪ $

Prepare to queue for a table at this popular restaurant in Central, known for its succulent and meaty goose.

 Yung Kee
MAP K5 ▪ 32–40 Wellington St ▪ 2522 1624 ▪ $$$

From its headset-toting waitresses to its efficient poultry kitchen (try the roast goose), Yung Kee is a riotous operation.

Caprice
MAP L4 ▪ 6/F Four Seasons Hotel, 8 Finance St ▪ 3196 8888 ▪ $$$

Head chef Guillaume Galliot and his team prepare modern French food in an open kitchen at this three Michelin-starred restaurant (see p54).

 Kau Kee
MAP J5 ▪ 21 Gough St ▪ 2850 5967 ▪ No credit cards ▪ Closed Sun ▪ $

Humble Kau Kee was once offered millions of dollars for its beef brisket noodle recipe. Taste it and see why. This is a place of pilgrimage for foodies around the city and beyond.

See map on pp64–5 ←

TOP 10 Hong Kong Island – Northeast

The east of the island was the first to take up the population pressures of the nascent colonial

The famous Noonday Gun

capital of Victoria, and until the late 1970s, parts of it had a seedy reputation. Some of that survives in the many pole-dancing clubs and tattoo parlours of Wan Chai, where Richard Mason wrote *The World of Suzie Wong* and generations of sailors have nursed hangovers. But today, you're more likely to run into Starbucks®. You'll see Hong Kongers mingling at the Happy Valley night races, or at Causeway Bay, lit by the neon of restaurants and boutiques. There are surprises among the warehouses and offices of Quarry Bay and Wan Chai – live jazz, dive bars and dance clubs.

HONG KONG ISLAND – NORTHEAST

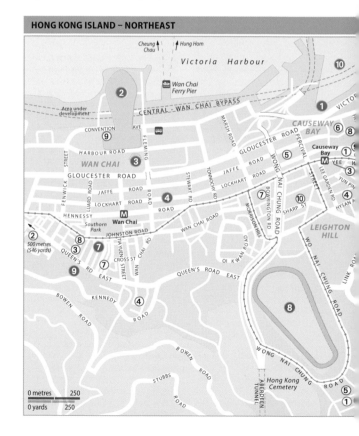

1 Noonday Gun

MAP Q5 ■ Waterfront near the Causeway Bay typhoon shelter ■ To fire gun (HK$33,000): 2599 6111

Immortalized in British playright and musician Noël Coward's famous song titled *Mad Dogs and Englishmen*, this famous cannon has been fired at midday every day since 1860. Some pay for the privilege of firing it, with the money going to charity. Otherwise, a gunner dressed in traditional military attire does the honours.

2 Convention and Exhibition Centre

MAP N5 ■ 1 Expo Dr, Wan Chai ■ 2582 8888 ■ www.hkcec.com

This building looks a bit like the Sydney Opera House might if its roof

Convention and Exhibition Centre

had just been swatted by a giant hammer. The vision of its designers was that the flowing lines would evoke a bird in flight. It is certainly a study in contrast, with the upthrust towers scratching the sky all around it. There was a race against time to complete stage two of the $5 billion complex in time for the 1997 Handover ceremony. Britain's loss and China's gain is commemorated with a big black obelisk. The centre also serves as a venue for occasional rave parties as well as a number of pop concerts.

3 Central Plaza

MAP N5 ■ 18 Harbour Rd, Wan Chai

Perhaps the developers figured "Central Plaza" had more cachet than "Wan Chai Plaza", or perhaps Wan Chai is central if you're talking about the mid-point of the waterfront. Anyway, Central Plaza (*see p39*) is Hong Kong's third-tallest building (after ICC Tower and Two IFC Tower), standing at 374 m (1,227 ft).

4 Lockhart Road

MAP M–P6

Made famous in Richard Mason's novel *The World of Suzie Wong*, Wan Chai's sinful strip has evolved into an attractive melting pot of cultures. Here, you will find down-at-heel discos, mock-British pubs, noon-time happy hour deals and super-trendy bars and restaurants. The road is almost always being dug up, which ultimately adds to the hubbub.

Statues of different gods at the Tin Hau Temple

⑤ Tin Hau Temple
MAP R6 ■ 10 Tin Hau Temple Rd, Causeway Bay ■ 2879 5612 ■ Open 7am–5pm daily

Not the biggest or best-known temple to the Chinese sea goddess, but certainly the most accessible. This was once the waterfront, believe it or not. There is usually a handful of worshippers burning incense and paying respects, although it may be packed during Chinese festivals.

⑥ Victoria Park
MAP Q–R5

Hong Kong's largest urban park *(see p43)* opened in 1957 and features a statue of the British monarch, which an "art activist" once redecorated with red paint. There are tennis courts,

SUN, MOON AND STAR STREETS

Hong Kong's history is reflected in its bilingual street names. For some streets the pronunciation is simply transliterated from Chinese to English, or the other way. Other streets have names whose meaning is translated, while some have two unrelated names. Wandering around Wan Chai you may come across Sun Street, Moon Street and Star Street, and branching off them is Electric Street. The latter was the site of a power station which began operations in 1890. Sun, Moon and Star Streets provided accommodation to the workers.

lawn bowling greens and a swimming pool. It's also the venue for many festivals and events, including the Chinese New Year Flower Market, as well as a number of political demonstrations, rallies and campaigns.

⑦ "Old" Wan Chai
MAP N6

This could almost be labelled Hong Kong's "Little Thailand". Dozens of Thai mini-marts and hole-in-the-wall Thai restaurants have sprung up amid Wan Chai market in the warren of lanes that run between Johnston Road and Queen's Road East. You can find the same dishes here for a quarter of what you'll pay in Thai restaurants just blocks away.

Skyscrapers around Victoria Park

8 Happy Valley Racecourse

From September to mid-July the thud of hooves on turf rings out most Wednesday nights from this famous racetrack (see pp16–17), which was once a malaria-ridden swamp. Here, people wager more money per meeting than at any other track in the world, but most locals come for the live music and to mingle.

9 Hopewell Centre

MAP N6 ■ 183 Queen's Rd E, Wan Chai ■ The Grand Buffet: 2506 0888 ■ www.hopewellcentre.com

Construction mogul Gordon Wu has built roads throughout China and half-built a railway in Bangkok, but Hopewell Centre remains his best-known edifice. The 64-storey cylinder makes diners dizzy in its revolving restaurant, The Grand Buffet, which, aside from the view, features one of the best buffet spreads in Hong Kong. Nighttimes are most spectacular so be sure to book well in advance.

10 Causeway Bay Typhoon Shelter

MAP Q5

Multimillion-dollar yachts call this packed haven home, a respite from the "big winds" that regularly bear down on the South China coast. There are also houseboats with homely touches like flower boxes permanently anchored behind the stone breakwater. The impressive edifice to the left as you look out to sea is the Royal Hong Kong Yacht Club.

Causeway Bay Typhoon Shelter

A DAY IN NORTHEAST HONG KONG ISLAND

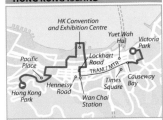

▶ MORNING

Start off with a stroll through **Hong Kong Park** (see p65), a green haven surrounded on all sides by thrusting towers of glass and concrete. Chances are you'll see several well-dressed couples awaiting their turn to be married at the Cotton Tree Drive Marriage Registry. Spend some time looking through the Edward Youde Aviary, a spectacular creation of mesh arches replete with Southeast Asian birdlife.

Make your way past Citibank's imposing black towers to **Pacific Place** (2844 8988) for a coffee and some shopping. Keep heading towards the harbour and you will see to your right the elegant sweep of the **HK Convention and Exhibition Centre** (see p73). Enjoy the harbour panorama through soaring glass walls.

AFTERNOON

Return to Wan Chai for lunch. **Lockhart Road** (see p73) is as good a place as any. Tucked away amid the bars are several small restaurants (see p77) with decent pub grub, as well as a variety of Thai, Mexican and Chinese food on offer.

Hennessy Road is the place to jump on a tram to **Causeway Bay**, due east of Wan Chai, or you may prefer to go one stop on the MTR. If you want to go shopping, take the Times Square exit, and start exploring from there. Then leave the crush and chaos behind with a leisurely afternoon stroll through **Victoria Park**, before wandering west for a Cantonese seafood dinner at **Yuet Wah Hui** (see p77).

See map on pp72–3

Places to Shop

Sogo Japanese department store

1 Sogo
MAP P6 ■ East Point Centre, Hennessy Rd, Causeway Bay

With a fine range of mostly Japanese goods, Sogo is very popular among locals. Stock up on Japanese food in the basement supermarket.

2 Aeon
MAP F5 ■ Kornhill Plaza, 2 Kornhill Rd, Quarry Bay

One of the biggest department-store chains. Lower rents to the east of the island translate into cheaper fashion, food and household goods.

3 Eslite
MAP N6 ■ Hysan Place, 500 Hennessy Rd, Causeway Bay

The largest bookstore in town and the first overseas branch of the Taiwanese chain famous for staying open till late at night. It also stocks stationery, gadgets and music.

4 Lee Gardens
MAP Q6 ■ 33 Hysan Ave, Causeway Bay

Hermès, Ralph Lauren Children, Chanel, Christian Dior and Cartier all reside here; Lee Gardens is the one-stop shop for the well-heeled.

5 Mezzanine
MAP E5 ■ 13–15 Yik Yam St, Happy Valley

Fashion designer to the stars Vivian Luk has opened her own couture store offering Oscar-style evening and especially bridal gowns.

6 D-mop
MAP Q5 ■ Shop 3, 2–4 Kingston St, Causeway Bay

Cool multi-brand store carrying popular fashion-forward Japanese labels, such as moussy, SLY, and BLACK, as well as its own collection of clothing and accessories.

7 Spring Garden Lane
MAP N6 ■ Spring Garden Lane, Wan Chai

Head to this fun market for a bargain. Export-quality clothing is sold at rock-bottom prices.

8 Good Old Days
MAP P5 ■ 4/F World Trade Centre, Causeway Bay

A reminder of how quirky Hong Kong can be, this tiny store sells nothing but vintage classic watches.

9 Island Beverley
MAP Q5 ■ 1 Great George St, Causeway Bay

An arcane arcade stuffed with tiny boutiques featuring the creations of Japanese and Korean designers.

10 Fortress
MAP P6 ■ 7/F & 8/F Times Square, 1 Matheson St, Causeway Bay

This is the best chain to buy the latest electronics, sold at reasonable prices and with reliable guarantees.

Fortress electronics store

Places to Eat and Drink

PRICE CATEGORIES

For a three-course meal for one with half
a bottle of wine and extra charges. Prices
are quoted in Hong Kong dollars.

$ under $250 $$ $250–600 $$$ over $600

1 Tasty Congee and Noodle Wantun Shop

MAP Q7 ▪ G/F, 21 King Kwong St,
Happy Valley ▪ 2838 3922 ▪ $

One of the best places to go for beef
fried noodles and piping-hot *congee*
(rice porridge). Try the dim sum too.

2 Petrus

MAP M6 ▪ 56/F Island
Shangri-La Hong Kong, Pacific
Place, 88 Queensway, Admiralty
▪ 2820 8590 ▪ $$$

This restaurant serves contemporary
French cuisine and has fantastic
panoramic views of the harbour.

Elegant interior at Petrus

3 22 Ships

MAP N6 ▪ 22 Ship St,
Wan Chai ▪ 2555 0722 ▪ $$$

One of Hong Kong's hottest tables
for modern tapas creations by
Jason Atherton. No reservations.

4 Tai Lung Fung

MAP N6 ▪ 5 Hing Wan St,
Wan Chai ▪ 2572 0055 ▪ $

This quirky local bar with an
old-school Hong Kong decor
attracts a young clientele.

5 Yuet Wah Hui

MAP P6 ▪ 2/F–3/F Chung
Wai Bldg, Lockhart Rd, Causeway
Bay ▪ 2394 9928 ▪ $$

A favourite among locals, this
Guangdong-style seafood restau-
rant is famous for its stir-fried
crab and glass noodles.

6 Kung Tak Lam

MAP P5 ▪ World Trade Center
1001, 280 Gloucester Rd, Causeway
Bay ▪ 2890 3127 ▪ $$

Good vegetarian restaurants can
be hard to find in Hong Kong.
The light, Shanghainese-style
dishes here stand out from the
competition *(see p54)*.

7 DimDimSum Dim Sum Specialty Store

MAP P6 ▪ 9 Tin Lok Lane, Wan Chai
▪ 2891 7677 ▪ $

Get a hearty, inexpensive dim sum
fix at this Wan Chai restaurant.

8 Bo Innovation

MAP N6 ▪ 2/F J Residence,
60 Johnston Rd, Wan Chai ▪ 2850
8371 ▪ $$$

Awarded three Michelin stars, this
highly modern Chinese restaurant
attracts a hip clientele.

9 One Harbour Road

MAP N5 ▪ Grand Hyatt, 1
Harbour Rd, Wan Chai ▪ 2584 7722
▪ Closed Sun ▪ $$$

For home-style Cantonese food at
its most pure and subtle, with no
fancy attempts at fusion, head
to One Harbour Road.

10 Classified

MAP Q7 ▪ 13 Yuk Sau St,
Happy Valley ▪ 2857 3454 ▪ $$

Happy Valley features a variety of
trendy wine bars and chic restau-
rants, including this outpost of
the famous chain serving freshly-
baked bread, artisan cheeses,
gourmet coffee and a range of
specialist wines.

See map on pp72–3

TOP 10 Hong Kong Island – South

Dolphin topiary, Ocean Park

Despite the slow creep of floodlit housing estates to the east and west, the south of Hong Kong Island (or "Southside" as everyone calls it) retains more than enough rugged coastline, wooded upland and sequestered beach to startle anyone whose preconception of Hong Kong was wholly urban. Traffic from the city passes through the Aberdeen Tunnel and enters a bright and shiny landscape of golf clubs, opulent homes and marinas. There is good swimming at Repulse and Deep Water bays, and even, at Big Wave Bay, some acceptable surf. Over at Stanley, stallholders set out their coral beads and antique opium pipes, while at isolated Shek O, media types snap up beachfront village houses. The Dragon's Back ridge, plunging down the southeast corner, offers some of the island's best walking.

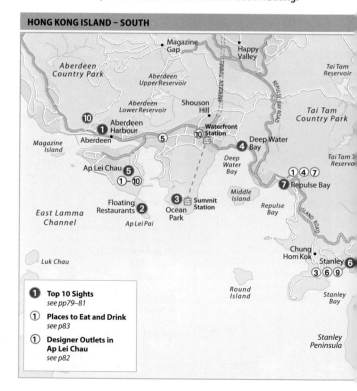

HONG KONG ISLAND – SOUTH

- Magazine Gap
- Happy Valley
- Aberdeen Country Park
- Tai Tam Reservoir
- Aberdeen Upper Reservoir
- Aberdeen Lower Reservoir
- Shouson Hill
- Tai Tam Country Park
- **10** Aberdeen Harbour
- Waterfront **10** Station
- Magazine Island
- **1** Aberdeen
- **5**
- Deep Water Bay
- Tai Tam T Reservo
- Ap Lei Chau **5**
- **1**–**10**
- Deep Water Bay
- **1 4 7**
- **7** Repulse Bay
- East Lamma Channel
- Floating Restaurants **2**
- **3** Summit Station
- Ocean Park
- Middle Island
- Repulse Bay
- Ap Lei Pai
- Luk Chau
- Chung Hom Kok
- Stanley **6**
- **3 6 9**
- Round Island
- Stanley Bay
- Stanley Peninsula

1 Top 10 Sights
see pp79–81

1 Places to Eat and Drink
see p83

1 Designer Outlets in Ap Lei Chau
see p82

Aberdeen Harbour
MAP E5

Residential blocks crowd Aberdeen's small, lovely harbour, which is still filled with high-prowed, wooden fishing boats, despite the fact that overfishing and pollution have decimated the Hong Kong fishing industry. Swerve the town centre and instead photograph the tyre-festooned sampans, or walk to the busy wholesale fish market at the western end of the harbour and watch the catches being loaded onto trucks and vans.

Ap Lei Pai
MAP E5

Experienced hikers will relish lacing up their boots to tackle Ap Lei Pai, a small island in Hong Kong's south side. Instead of doing the full route from Ap Lei Chau

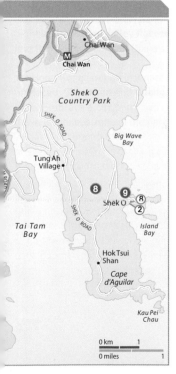

(see p80), grab a sampan from Aberdeen Harbour and have it drop you off at the base of the island. Then, scramble up the rocks to reach the tip of Ap Lei Pai, where stunning coastal views await. While it's a short trek at just under an hour, it involves some technical difficulty – there are ropes coming down to help you on the steep parts, for example. Wearing gloves is advised.

Hiking from Ap Lei Chau to Ap Lei Pai

Ocean Park
MAP E5 ■ 3923 2323 ■ Open times vary; check website for details ■ Adm ■ www.oceanpark.com.hk

This long-established theme park (see p48) responded to the arrival of Disneyland on Lantau Island with a major refurbishment and a corresponding surge in popularity. There are more than enough attractions in the park to keep children and adults busy for a whole day. You'll find tons of rides, many dining options, and aquatic displays, such as Atoll Reef, which recreates the habitats and sea life of a coral reef and is a great way to learn about wildlife conservation.

Deep Water Bay
MAP E5

There's an almost Mediterranean air to the lovely beach and waterfront of Deep Water Bay, a popular place for beach lovers and the well-to-do who settle in the Bay's upmarket housing. The smallish beach is protected by lifeguards and a shark net, and the water is usually clean. As with most beaches in Hong Kong, it gets crowded in fine weather.

5 Ap Lei Chau
MAP E5

Supposedly the most densely populated island in the world, Ap Lei Chau (or Duck Tongue Island), opposite the Aberdeen waterfront, is crowded with a forest of high-rise apartment buildings. Bargain hunters may find a visit to the many discount outlets housed in Horizon Plaza (see p82) worthwhile. Close to the ferry pier lie family businesses, boatyards and temples that have survived the modern developments.

6 Stanley

Formerly a busy fishing village, Stanley (see pp20–21) was one of the largest towns on the island before the British arrived and placed a fort on its strategic peninsula. A number of relics from both eras remain, but Stanley's many excellent seaside restaurants, picturesque promenades and extensive market are justifiably the main draws for visitors. From here, it's also a short ferry ride to Po Toi Island (see p119), known for its breathtaking scenery.

7 Repulse Bay
MAP F5

Another popular destination, Repulse Bay's beach is clean and well-tended, if sometimes over-crowded with thousands of visitors. Eating and drinking choices range from small cafés on the beach to

The Verandah (see p83), a classy restaurant run by the same group as the Peninsula Hotel in Tsim Sha Tsui. Try afternoon tea here. The Hong Kong Life Guards Club situated at the far southern end of the beach is also worth a look for its scores of statues of gods and fabulous beasts.

Walkers on the Dragon's Back ridge

8 Dragon's Back
MAP F5

This 6-km (4-mile) walk looks daunting on the map, but the route along the gently ascending ridge of the Dragon's Back will mean not too much huffing and puffing for the reasonably fit. The reward is unbeatable views down to the craggy coastline of the D'Aguilar Peninsula, Big Wave Bay and genteel Shek O. At a gentle pace the walk should take about 3 hours, enough time to have built up a good appetite when you arrive in Shek O. Take plenty of water, especially in the summer.

Repulse Bay

Rocky coastline, Shek O

9 Shek O
MAP F5

Remote and undeveloped, Shek O village is worth the relatively lengthy train and bus ride necessary to reach it. The serenity is upset only at weekends by droves of sun worshippers heading for its lovely beach. A short walk to the small headland leads to striking rock formations, pounding waves and cooling South China Sea breezes. Surfing and body boarding are often viable on Big Wave Bay, a short walk or taxi ride north. Make your way to the Cococabana (see p83), a lovely bar and Mediterranean-style restaurant, for a post-ramble drink and a bite to eat.

Steep steps at the Chinese Cemetery

10 Chinese Cemetery
MAP E5

Stretching away on the hill above Aberdeen, the Chinese Cemetery is a great place for taking photographs, both of the cemetery itself and of the harbour beneath. Note, however, that negotiating the steep, seemingly end-less steps is quite an undertaking, especially on a hot day.

A CIRCULAR TOUR

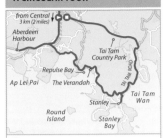

▶ **MORNING**

This circular tour of Hong Kong Island is perfectly feasible in one day if you start early enough.

From Central, jump on an Aberdeen-bound bus, alighting close to **Aberdeen Harbour** (see p79). Haggle for a sampan harbour tour offered by one of the touts on the waterfront. Take in the sights of one of Hong Kong's oldest fishing villages and keep a look out for Aberdeen's few remaining houseboats.

Opt for a leisurely lunch at **Repulse Bay**, which is just a 15-minute bus ride away. Enjoy the beach and a swim, then eat either at one of the beachfront cafés or upmarket **The Verandah** (see p83). Alternatively, head to the supermarket near The Verandah and have your own picnic to enjoy on the beach.

AFTERNOON

Just a short hop further south along the coast, the lovely town of **Stanley** is certainly worth a visit. If you haven't yet eaten, the restaurants here are excellent, some with sea views. Spend a couple of hours browsing for clothes and souvenirs to take home in **Stanley market** (see pp20–21).

If you're in the mood for a refreshing walk, take a short bus or taxi ride to **Tai Tam Country Park**, accessed off the Tai Tam Road. A path leads through to Wong Nai Chung Gap, from where buses and taxis head back into the city.

See map on pp78–9 ⬅

Designer Outlets in Ap Lei Chau

1 Horizon Plaza
MAP E5 ■ 2 Lee Wing St, Ap Lei Chau

This shabby, high-rise building on the edge of the island of Ap Lei Chau (see p80) is home to a number of outlets for discount clothing such as Replay, and warehouse furniture and home furnishings such as Indigo Living. Start with an energizing coffee from the café in Tree on the top floor, before making your way down through the many stores. A taxi from Aberdeen is perhaps the simplest way to reach it.

2 Joyce Warehouse
21/F Horizon Plaza

The extensive selection of clearance designer wear from the stores of Hong Kong chain Joyce are perhaps the main reward for struggling out to Horizon Plaza. You get discounts of 60 per cent on the likes of Armani.

3 Agnes B Outlet
18/F Horizon Plaza

This French designer brand is known for its classy selection of smart casual wear for all. Check out the accessories line, too.

4 Kate Spade
17/F Horizon Plaza

Fans of the high street New York brand will delight in this outlet, offering steep discounts on the brand's colourful clothes and accessories.

5 The Birdcage
16/F Horizon Plaza

This one offers mostly original Chinese antiques and curios sourced by the owners of the quirky Birdcage shop on the mainland. Items range from portable antiques and collectables to furniture.

6 i.t.
21/F Horizon Plaza

Off-season contemporary fashion lines by emerging Asian designers are sold here at discount prices.

Shoppers at Lane Crawford Outlet

7 Lane Crawford Outlet
25/F Horizon Plaza

Slow-moving items and old stock from Hong Kong's trendy department store are on sale here at lower than original prices.

8 Shanghai Tang
18/F Horizon Plaza

Find craftsmanship and unique designs at this luxury fashion house. While Shanghai Tang has locations worldwide, it's a Hong Kong born-and-bred brand, with a decent range of traditional Chinese clothing and kitchenware.

9 Indigo Living
6/F Horizon Plaza

Indigo does contemporary furniture and homewares with an Asian twist, with Indigo Kids the place for children's bedrooms and nursery furniture at a discount. They also offer design consultancy and furniture rental services.

10 Ralph Lauren Factory Outlet
18/F Horizon Plaza

Choose from a range of last season's accessories and clothes by powerhouse Ralph Lauren. This is one of several outlets scattered through the Horizon Plaza mall.

Places to Eat and Drink

PRICE CATEGORIES

For a three-course meal for one with half a bottle of wine and extra charges. Prices are quoted in Hong Kong dollars.

$ under $250 $$ $250–600 $$$ over $600

1 The Verandah
MAP F5 ■ 109 Repulse Bay Rd, Repulse Bay ■ 2292 2822 ■ Closed Mon & Tue ■ $$$

Indisputably Southside's premier venue, The Verandah (see p55), with its sea views and old colonial grandeur, is the place for big-budget romancing.

2 Cococabana
MAP F5 ■ G/F, Shek O Beach Bldg, Shek O Village ■ 2812 2226 ■ $$

Located in the tiny bohemian enclave of Shek O and overlooking the beach, this restaurant serves Provençal food. Although this is not a cheap option, the service can be slow.

3 Pickled Pelican
MAP F6 ■ 90 Stanley Main St, Stanley ■ 2813 4313 ■ Closed Tue ■ $$

Reliable, tasty English pub food is served with speciality beers and a wide choice of Scotch whiskies here.

Outdoor seating, Pickled Pelican

4 Spices
MAP F5 ■ G/F The Arcade, 109 Repulse Bay Rd, Repulse Bay ■ 2292 2821 ■ $$

One of the best places for alfresco dining in Hong Kong, Spices (see p55) serves well-executed Thai and Indian curries in a lush garden setting. Expect a relaxed atmosphere and good service.

5 Nam Long Shan Cooked Food Market
MAP E5 ■ 1 Nam Long Shan Rd ■ 2553 3730 ■ $

Usually located above market buildings, cooked food courts are an affordable way to try a host of cuisines. The food stalls at Nam Long Shan serve everything from Cantonese stir-fry to Thai food.

6 Ocean Rock Seafood & Tapas
MAP F6 ■ 102 Murray House, Stanley Plaza ■ 2899 0858 ■ $$

End a satisfying day in Stanley at this atmospheric Spanish restaurant. Romantics will gravitate towards the balcony tables at sunset.

7 Amalfitana Artisan Pizza Bar
MAP F5 ■ Shop 105, The Pulse, 28 Beach Rd, Repulse Bay ■ 2388 7787 ■ $$

This breezy restaurant serves one of the best pizzas in the area. It also has a good selection of cocktails.

8 Happy Garden
MAP F5 ■ 786 Shek O Village ■ 2809 4165 ■ $

Long running Thai canteen offering, excellent *pad thai* and satay.

9 Smuggler's Inn
MAP F6 ■ 90A Stanley Main St ■ 2813 8852 ■ $

Stanley's gentrification has bypassed this place, which is a relic of the days when British soldiers from Stanley Fort blew half their wages here.

10 Canton Bistro
MAP E5 ■ G/F, Hong Kong Ocean Park Marriott Hotel, 180 Wong Chuk Hang Rd, Aberdeen ■ 3555 1910 ■ $$

Dig into freshly prepared dim sum at this elegant restaurant.

See map on pp78–9

🔟 Tsim Sha Tsui

On one level, Tsim Sha Tsui (universally truncated to "TST" in a gesture to non-Cantonese speakers), with its salesmen touting goods to visitors, is a textbook tourist district. But there is also much more to it than that. Here you'll find a profusion of world-class cultural venues, galleries and museums, such as the Museum of History and the Science Museum. There are also magnificent hotels – the Langham, the Peninsula, the InterContinental – of jaw-dropping luxury. And every product and service the human mind can conceive of can be found in the monolithic Harbour City shopping mall.

Exhibit at the Museum of History

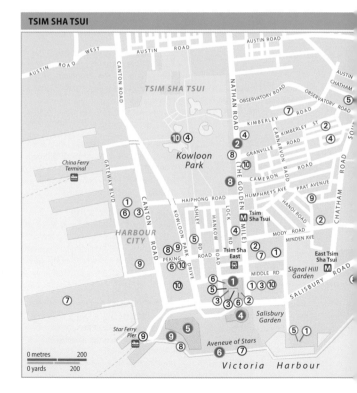

TSIM SHA TSUI

1 The Peninsula

The last word in luxury service and accommodation. This venerable hotel sits like a proud old dowager, gazing sedately across at the vertiginous Hong Kong Island skyline. The cheapest rooms start where many other luxury hotels stop, however, special offers sometimes apply. A night in the opulent Peninsula suite will set you back almost the price of a small car. It has eight bars and restaurants, including the Philippe Starck-designed Felix and French stalwart Gaddi's *(see p91)*. If you desire, you can swoop onto the roof by helicopter or be collected by Rolls-Royce *(see p149)*.

2 The Golden Mile
MAP N1–4

This strip that stretches up Nathan Road from the waterfront could be

Neon signs on the Golden Mile

more accurately dubbed the "neon mile". It is less glitzy than Central and comprises mainly bars, restaurants, tailors, camera and electronic shops and the odd desultory topless bar. The crowds are sometimes so great that walking the Golden Mile becomes a major challenge.

3 Museum of History
MAP P2 ■ 100 Chatham Rd S ■ 2724 9042 ■ Open 10am–6pm Mon & Wed–Fri, 10am–7pm Sat & Sun ■ Adm (for exhibitions)

This museum was built at a cost of almost HK$390 million, half of which was spent on its *pièce de résistance*, the Hong Kong Story, which attempts to chronicle the 400 million-odd years since Hong Kong coalesced from the primordial ooze. The story is told across eight galleries containing more than 4,000 exhibits, which vividly outline the natural environment, folk culture and historical development of Hong Kong.

4 Space Museum
MAP N4 ■ Cultural Centre Complex, 10 Salisbury Rd ■ 2721 0226 ■ Open 10am–9pm Sat & Sun, 1–9pm Mon & Wed–Fri ■ Adm (free Wed)

When you've had enough of history, come and peek into the future. This odd-looking dome in the heart of Tsim Sha Tsui includes an Omnimax theatre and interactive exhibits.

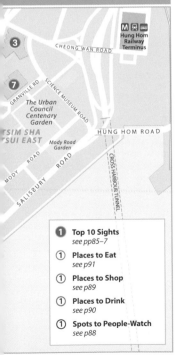

Map labels:

M R Hung Hom Railway Terminus

CHEONG WAN ROAD

3

7

GRANVILLE RD

SCIENCE MUSEUM ROAD

The Urban Council Centenary Garden

TSIM SHA TSUI EAST

Mody Road Garden

HUNG HOM ROAD

MODY ROAD

CROSS HARBOUR TUNNEL

SALISBURY ROAD

1 Top 10 Sights
see pp85–7

1 Places to Eat
see p91

1 Places to Shop
see p89

1 Places to Drink
see p90

1 Spots to People-Watch
see p88

The monolithic Cultural Centre with the clock tower in front

⑤ Cultural Centre

MAP M–N4 ▪ 10 Salisbury Rd
▪ 2734 2009 ▪ Open 9am–11pm
daily; box office: 10am–6:30pm
Sun–Thu (to 8pm Fri & Sat)

With a peerless view beckoning across the water, those in charge decided to build the world's first windowless building, and covered it in public toilet-style pink tiles. Wander around and marvel at one of the great architectural debacles of the 20th century. It hosts some good dance and theatre productions, as well as some free foyer performances.

⑥ Avenue of Stars

MAP N4 ▪ Tsim Sha Tsui
Promenade ▪ www.avenueof
stars.com.hk/en

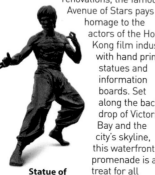

Reopened in 2019 after extensive renovations, the famous Avenue of Stars pays homage to the actors of the Hong Kong film industry with hand prints, statues and information boards. Set along the back-drop of Victoria Bay and the city's skyline, this waterfront promenade is a treat for all cinephiles.

Statue of Bruce Lee

⑦ Science Museum

MAP P3 ▪ 2 Science Museum
Rd ▪ 2732 3232 ▪ Open 10am–9pm
Sat & Sun, 10am–7pm Mon–Wed & Fri
▪ Adm (free Wed) ▪ www.lcsd.gov.hk

There are some fascinating interactive displays here if you don't mind fighting your way through the giggling, pushing throngs of schoolchildren. There are enough buttons to push, gadgets to grapple with and levers to tweak to satisfy even the most hard-to-please kids. Basic principles of science are explained in an entertaining manner, inviting hands-on exploration for both the young and young-at-heart.

⑧ Kowloon Mosque

MAP N3 ▪ 105 Nathan Rd
▪ 2724 0095 ▪ Open 5am–10pm daily
▪ Jumah (Friday) prayers at 1:15pm

When the muezzin calls the faithful to prayer, the Jamia Masjid Islamic Centre is where you'll find most of Hong Kong's Muslims. You can stop by for a look, but take your shoes off and be respectful. Entry to the inner part is not permitted unless you are a Muslim coming for prayer.

⑨ Clock Tower

MAP M4

The Kowloon-Canton Railway, which now ends at Hung Hom, used to finish at this clock tower (see p18), as did the rather more famous Orient Express. From here,

CHUNGKING MANSIONS

A hub for South Asian and African communities in Hong Kong, this 17-storey building is worth a visit if you're in Tsim Sha Tsui. The massive maze of a building is known for its fast-turnover shops, canteens and hustlers crowding its lobby, and the warren of cramped, budget accommodation (see p59) filling the upper floors. But if you're after a dirt-cheap suitcase for those unplanned purchases, a discount phone-card or plug adaptor, or superb Indian food, Chungking Mansions (see p152) can deliver.

you can walk for more than a kilometre around the Tsim Sha Tsui waterfront and spot the occasional optimistic fisherman dangling a line in the harbour.

10 Kowloon Park
MAP M–N3 ■ Haiphong Rd
■ Open 5am–midnight daily

If the multitudes of hawkers in Tsim Sha Tsui become too much for you, then venture through the gates of Kowloon Park (see p49) to find a well-shaded bench and watch the world go by. There is an aviary and a pond with flamingos and other aquatic birdlife as well as martial arts and lion dance performances on Sundays, when the park tends to get busy.

Picturesque Kowloon Park

A MORNING OUT

▶ MORNING

Catch the **Star Ferry** (see pp18–19) to Tsim Sha Tsui.

As you come in, check out the vast West Kowloon Reclamation site to the left, home of the shiny, silver **International Commerce Centre** (see p38). The 108-floor monolith houses hotels, apartments and a viewing deck.

The ferry ride takes a brisk 10 minutes. Once you disembark at the historic Star Ferry Pier, saunter past the old **Clock Tower**, pause to take in one of the world's most breathtaking views, then turn right and stroll along the waterfront **Avenue of Stars**.

From here, brave the crush and bustle of **The Golden Mile** (see p85). As you shop or window shop at the rows of stores along the strip, expect to be approached by zealous tailors offering visitors various suits and dresses at slashed prices.

AFTERNOON

When you've had enough of the smog-shrouded streets, hawkers and being jostled, cross Haiphong Road into **Kowloon Park**. There is plenty of space here to take a breather and do some serious people-watching.

You'll probably be getting peckish by now. Head back down Nathan Road to one of the excellent Indian restaurants in **Chungking Mansions**, or for something less hectic, **The Peninsula** (see p149) has a host of culinary options.

See map on pp84–5 ←

Spots to People-Watch

1 Tao Heung
MAP N3 ■ Star Mansion,
3 Minden Rd ■ 8300 8084 ■ $

Come here early and join the Cantonese at their best – tucking into a tasty, fresh and made-to-order dim sum breakfast with their families, or just sitting quietly with a pot of tea and a newspaper.

Visitors at Tao Heung

2 Chungking Mansions
One of the most popular "mansions", the Chungking Mansions (see p87) is known for its Indian and Pakistani food and community vibe.

3 The Lobby at The Peninsula
Opulent Neo-Classical setting at this hotel (see p149) makes for a rather fabulous afternoon tea with the territory's smart set: scones, cucumber sandwiches, petit fours, a string quartet, the works.

4 Kowloon Park
One of the best places (see p87) in all Hong Kong to visit at dawn, when tai chi and martial arts practitioners hone their skills among the sculptures and fig trees.

5 Felix
Settle down with a drink at the bar, or explore the menu at Felix (see p91). Soak up the atmosphere and the sweeping views of Victoria Harbour.

6 Harbour City
A people-watcher's paradise. This massive labyrinth of interconnected malls has plenty of cafés and benches from which to enjoy the world passing by.

7 Waterfront Promenade
MAP M–N4 ■ Salisbury Rd

Walking east from the Star Ferry, you will meet tai chi adepts, culture vultures and local ladies with their tiny dogs. The promenade is very popular for the harbour's A Symphony of Lights show, at 8pm daily.

8 The Langham Hotel
MAP M4 ■ 8 Peking Rd
■ 2375 1133

Understated and elegant, the Langham attracts similar clientele, such as screen star Michelle Yeoh, perhaps on her way to T'ang Court.

9 Star Ferry Piers
MAP M4

Inspiring places to take in Hong Kong's bustle and watch the iconic ferries and their passengers.

10 Heritage 1881
MAP M4 ■ 2A Canton Rd

Heritage 1881 is the name given to the super-swanky, revamped former Hong Kong Marine Police headquarters. It features a boutique hotel, bars and restaurants, and designer shops attracting smart customers.

Boutiques at Heritage 1881

For a key to restaurant price ranges see p91

Places to Shop

Harbour City shopping mall

1 Harbour City
MAP M3–4 ▪ Canton Rd

There are at least 450 shops in this vast agglomeration of malls stretching the length of Canton Road. It comprises the Ocean Terminal, Ocean Centre and Golden Gateway complexes.

2 Granville Road
MAP N3

Great for souvenir T-shirts, all manner of big-label knock-offs and factory seconds, as well as good-value clothing and accessories from chain stores.

3 Joyce
MAP N4 ▪ 3205 Gateway Arcade, Harbour City

Founder Joyce Ma is a Hong Kong fashion icon. Her flagship store is in Central, however. the Harbour City outlet is also impressive.

4 Rise Commercial Building
MAP N3 ▪ 5–11 Granville Circuit

Each shop inside this mall has a character of its own. You will find clothes and accessories as well as gifting options here.

5 Beverley Commercial Centre
MAP N3 ▪ 87–105 Chatham Rd S

The original beacon of cool in Tsim Sha Tsui, with floor after floor of mini-boutiques from local designers.

6 The Peninsula Hong Kong Arcade
MAP N4 ▪ 1–17 Nathan Rd, Kowloon

A selection of fashionable designer boutiques, jewellers and bespoke tailors is located in the arcade of Peninsula Hotel (see p149).

7 Toys 'R' Us
MAP M4 ▪ Shop OTG21–24 & OTG39–42, Ocean Terminal

Possibly the biggest branch in Hong Kong – a definite favourite for kids.

8 Chow Tai Fook
MAP N3 ▪ Park Lane Shopper's Boulevard, 123 Nathan Rd

One of Hong Kong's major jewellery chains, home to a dazzling display of gold, silver, jewels and price tags.

Chow Tai Fook jewellery store

9 Fortress
MAP M4 ▪ Shop 335–7, Level 3, Ocean Centre

If you're after electronic goods and baffled by the sheer number of shops around TST, chain-store Fortress is a good bet. Other shops may advertise cheaper prices, but not all dealers are honest.

10 Sam's Tailor
MAP N3 ▪ Burlington Arcade, 94 Nathan Rd

Portraits of former clients, including princes, presidents and pop stars, look on as the third generation of the Melwani family measures you for a well-priced, well-fitting suit that will be ready in two to three days.

See map on pp84–5

Places to Drink

The Lobby Lounge, with superb views across the harbour

1 The Lobby Lounge
MAP N4 ■ 18 Salisbury Rd

Some of the best harbour views in Hong Kong are to be found in the bar of the superb Hotel InterContinental *(see p148)*. The aspect more than make up for the price of the drinks.

2 Bar Butler
MAP N3 ■ 6/F, Mody House, 30 Mody Rd, Tsim Sha Tsui ■ 2724 3828

This snug, 18-seat whiskey bar offers a taste of Japan with its thoughtfully curated drinks.

3 The Bar
MAP N4 ■ 1/F The Peninsula Hotel

This upmarket watering hole serves as a delightful refuge from the Kowloon crowds – but prepare to pay through the nose for drinks.

4 Eyebar
MAP N4 ■ 30/F iSquare, 63 Nathan Rd

Uninterrupted Victoria Harbour views are highlighted with double-height windows and a telescope on the rooftop bar's terrace.

5 Ned Kelly's Last Stand
MAP N3 ■ 11A Ashley Rd

This place has been here forever, as has the jazz band. Come here for an opportunity to get your feet tapping to tunes by the crustiest, most grizzled bunch of musicians this side of New Orleans.

6 Aqua Spirit
MAP M4 ■ 29/F, 1 Peking Rd

Sit in a cubbyhole facing the window and sip a glass of bubbly as you watch the harbour light up.

7 Dada Bar & Lounge
MAP N3 ■ 2/F De Luxe Manor, 39 Kimberley Rd

A gorgeous cocktail and wine bar, Dada Lounge is decorated in truly over-the-top style with Alice in Wonderland over-sized chairs, chandeliers and horse-head motifs.

8 Aqua Luna
MAP N4 ■ Tsim Sha Tsui Pier 1

Lie back on your day bed with a drink in hon on the ultimate harbour cruise; the *Aqua Luna* is the last traditional vessel to be built in Hong Kong. Daily sailings depart from Tsim Sha Tsui Pier 1 *(see p40)*.

9 Fatt's Place
MAP N3 ■ G/F 2 Hart Ave

This casual beer bar has a great selection of international ales and lagers by the bottle or on tap. Happy hour runs from 3pm to 9pm daily.

10 Sky Lounge
MAP N4 ■ 18/F Sheraton Hotel, 20 Nathan Rd

Another very comfortable location from which to enjoy the nightly cross-harbour light show below with a glass of something chilled to hand.

Places to Eat

1 Oyster and Wine Bar
MAP N4 ▪ 18/F Sheraton Hotel,
20 Nathan Rd ▪ 2369 1111 ▪ $$$
A sublime view and oysters
so fresh they flinch when you
squeeze a lemon on them.

PRICE CATEGORIES
For a three-course meal for one with half
a bottle of wine and extra charges. Prices
are quoted in Hong Kong dollars.

$ under $250 $$ $250–600 $$$ over $600

2 Felix Restaurant
MAP N4 ▪ 28/F The Peninsula
Hotel ▪ 2696 6778 ▪ $$$
The cosmopolitan cuisine is fantastic,
the view is better and the rich and
famous throng the bar. Check out
the interesting Philippe Starck-
designed urinals, where you face
wall-to-ceiling glass windows and
get a stunning view of Hong Kong.

3 Morton's of Chicago
MAP N4 ▪ 4/F Sheraton Hotel
▪ 2732 2343 ▪ $$$
A carnivore's paradise. Huge slabs of
steak aged and cooked to perfection.

4 Cuisine, Cuisine
MAP N3 ▪ The Mira Hotel,
118 Nathan Rd ▪ 2315 5222 ▪ $$$
Michelin-recommended Cantonese
cuisine fuses modern and traditional
in an elegant setting.

5 Nobu
MAP N4 ▪ 2/F Hotel
InterContinental, 18 Salisbury Rd
▪ 2313 2323 ▪ $$$
Enjoy fine dining at one of the world's
most famous Japanese restaurants.

6 Gaddi's
MAP N4 ▪ 1/F The Peninsula
Hotel ▪ 2696 6763 ▪ $$$
Impeccable French cuisine,
irreproachable service and famous
patrons have earned Gaddi's (see
p55) its reputation as one of Asia's
finest restaurants.

7 The Delhi Club
MAP N4 ▪ Floor 3, Block C,
Chungking Mansions ▪ 2368 1682 ▪ $
A low-key setting for some superb,
inexpensive, filling Indian curries,
this is a worthy reason to push
through the touts and crowds
filling Chungking Mansions' lobby.

8 Wildfire
MAP N3 ▪ Avenue of Stars
▪ 3690 1598 ▪ $$
A great place for pizza and pasta,
Wildfire has terrace seating on
the Avenue of Stars making it a
popular weekend brunch spot.
Branches also at the Peak,
Causeway Bay and Sai Wan Ho.

9 T'ang Court
MAP N4 ▪ 1–2/F Langham
Hotel, 8 Peking Rd, Kowloon ▪ 2132
7898 ▪ $$$
This elegant restaurant is one of
the few in the city to gain its third
Michelin star. T'ang Court (see
p54) serves Cantonese delicacies.

10 Hutong
MAP M4 ▪ 28/F, 1 Peking Rd
▪ 3428 8342 ▪ $$$
Updated Northern Chinese classics
are served in this restaurant with
magnificent views. Try the signature
Red Lantern Crispy Soft Shell Crabs.

The bar at Nobu

See map on pp84–5

TOP 10 Yau Ma Tei, Mong Kok and Prince Edward

The tourist glitz of Tsim Sha Tsui fades when one travels north towards the neighbourhoods of Yau Ma Tei and Prince Edward. Densely populated even by Hong Kong standards, Mong Kok and Yau Ma Tei are always brimming with activity, and many of their busy streets are full of buzzing markets. To the north, where open fields once stood, is the district of Prince Edward, home to one of the largest sports stadiums in Kowloon. Come to this delightful heartland of Hong Kong to explore the variety of cuisines served at its numerous restaurants and to shop at the bustling market.

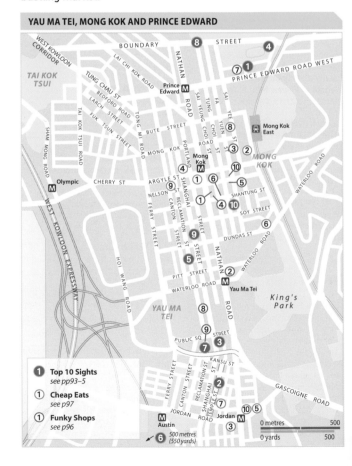

YAU MA TEI, MONG KOK AND PRINCE EDWARD

1 Top 10 Sights
  see pp93–5

1 Cheap Eats
  see p97

1 Funky Shops
  see p96

0 metres   500
0 yards   500

500 metres
(550 yards)

Stalls of colourful flowers at the Flower Market

1 Flower Market

Near Prince Edward is a vibrant flower market which is at its brightest in the morning. The stalls and shops lining the entire length of Flower Market Road sell a wide variety of flowers. It is a wonderfully colourful sight and a good place to take photographs. The market (see p57) is especially exciting to visit during the Chinese New Year celebrations (see p60).

2 Temple Street Night Market

Visit the chaotic, crowded night market on Temple Street (see pp22–3) as much for the spectacle as for the shopping experience.

3 Tin Hau Temple
MAP M1 ■ 2385 0759 ■ Open 8am–5pm daily ■ www.ctc.org.hk

The Tin Hau Temple in Yau Ma Tei is divided into three sections. Only one of these is actually devoted to Tin Hau, the sea goddess, who is Hong Kong's favourite deity and essentially its patron. Admittedly, it is neither the oldest nor the grandest temple in the territory, but it is pretty nonetheless. The other two sections are dedicated to Shing Wong, the god of the city, and To Tei, the god of the earth. Officially, no photography is allowed anywhere inside the temple. English-speaking visitors should head for a couple of stalls at the far end of the temple, where they can have their fortunes told in English.

4 Bird Garden
MAP E4 ■ Yuen Po St

The pretty Bird Garden is where local folk, mostly elderly, take their birds to sing and get some fresh air with other birds. Set up in 1997 for local bird lovers, it is laid out in the style of a traditional Chinese garden. Fresh bird food, in the form of live grasshoppers, is fed to the birds by their owners through the cage bars with chopsticks.

Bird cages in the Bird Garden

5 Reclamation Street Market
MAP E4 ■ Open 6am–5pm daily

If you haven't seen a Hong Kong produce market in full swing, you could do worse than wander down Reclamation Street. The market sells predominantly fresh fruit and vegetables, and will provide some good photo opportunities. The squeamish, however, may want to avoid wandering inside the municipal wet-market building where livestock is freshly slaughtered and expertly eviscerated on the spot.

6 West Kowloon Reclamation
MAP L1–3

The reclaimed land of West Kowloon is a jumble of road intersections and messy building sites, as planners argue over exactly what will fill it. Rising 484 m (1,588 ft) over everything, the huge International Commerce Centre (see p38) opened in 2010 as the tallest building in Hong Kong, topping Two IFC. Its sky100 Observation Deck provides the highest indoor viewing platform in the city, with great harbour views.

Jewellery stall, Jade Market

7 Jade Market
MAP M1 ■ Kansu St ■ Open 9am–5:45pm Mon–Sat

The small, covered Jade Market (see p57) is worth a quick forage even if you're not intending to buy any jade. Dozens of stalls sell jewellery, small animal figures (many representing characters from the Chinese zodiac) and beads in jade. There will be few bargains on sale, particularly to those without a knowledge of good jade, but there's plenty of cheap jade trinkets available for sale.

8 Boundary Street
MAP E4

History is visible in the ruler-straight line of Boundary Street (see p36), which marked the border between British Hong Kong and China between 1860 and 1898. The lower part of the Kowloon Peninsula was ceded (supposedly in perpetuity) by China to the British. The British then became worried over water shortages and wanted yet more land to protect Hong Kong Island from the threat of bombardment from newly invented long-range artillery. In 1898 the border was moved again to include the entire New Territories, this time on a 99-year lease.

International Commerce Centre

THE TRIADS

Overcrowded Mong Kok is the heartland of the Hong Kong triad gangs. The triads originated in 17th-century China as secret societies who tried to reinstall the Ming dynasty after the Manchus took over. Though they have been given a romantic image in literature and the cinema, the modern-day reality is a little grittier. However, tourists are unlikely to be a target and the area is a safe place to visit.

⑨ Shanghai Street
MAP E4

The whole area around Shanghai and Reclamation streets is a traditional Chinese neighbourhood, if somewhat less vibrant than it once was. Interesting nooks and shops include funeral parlours, herbalists, health-tea shops, paper-kite shops and, at 21 Ning Po Street, a shop selling pickled snakes.

⑩ Ladies' Market
MAP E4 ■ Open 11am–11:30pm daily

There is plenty more than women's clothing here (see p57). The shopping area consists of three parallel streets: Fa Yuen Street, crammed mostly with sports goods and trainer shops; Tung Choi Street (the former ladies' market); and Sa Yeung Choi Street, specializing in consumer electronics. Market-stall prices are cheap, and shop prices are better than those on Hong Kong Island. The crowds here can be tiring, though, especially on hot days.

Ladies' Market, Tung Choi Street

DOWN THE PENINSULA

▶ MORNING

Take the MTR to Prince Edward to start at the top of the Kowloon Peninsula, near the old Chinese border at **Boundary Street**. Take Exit B2 and head to the **Bird Garden** (see p93) via the flower shops and stalls in the **Flower Market** (see p93). Testament to the Chinese love of goldfish, the stalls at the top of Tung Choi Street sell a surprising variety of these pets.

Multitudes of cheap shops and market stalls are found a short walk away to the south on the streets below **Argyle Street** and east of **Nathan Road** (see p43). Pedestrians also abound – some 150,000 souls live in every square kilometre of this part.

Crossing Nathan Road, head to the **Jade Market** for jewellery and figurines. If you want the best choice of jade, arrive before lunchtime because some of the stallholders pack up after this.

AFTERNOON

Take a breather in the small, pleasant square across the way and watch the world go by with the elderly locals, or peep inside the busy **Tin Hau Temple** (see p93). Then break for a rough-and-ready cheap Chinese lunch in the covered canteens on the corner of **Pak Hoi** and **Temple Street**.

After lunch explore the produce stalls along **Reclamation Street Market** and the old Chinese district around **Shanghai Street**.

See map on p92 ←

Funky Shops

1 King Wah Centre
MAP E4 ■ 628 Nathan Rd

Head over to this uncrowded mall for street clothing, stylish accessories, handbags and watches. There is vintage denim and other 1970s and 1980s rarities, plus kitsch Japanese cartoon ephemera.

2 In's Point
MAP E4 ■ 530–538 Nathan Rd

Explore three floors of toy shops selling mostly Japanese anime figurines. There's also a LEGO® shop and one especially dedicated to the legendary martial artist, Bruce Lee.

3 Sasa Cosmetics
MAP E4 ■ 160 Sai Yeung Choi St South

Conveniently located outlet of an extensive Hong Kong chain selling cosmetics of every type at very low prices. Perfume is a bargain here.

4 Sim City
MAP E4 ■ Chung Kiu Commercial Bldg, 47–51 Shan Tung St

A three-floor haven for photography enthusiasts, Sim City comprises a number of shops selling cut-price camera gear. A bit of haggling can fetch you some excellent deals.

5 Mongkok Computer Centre
MAP E4 ■ 8A Nelson St

The deals on computer hardware and software are not as good as those in Sham Shui Po, but this is convenient for a huge selection of games and accessories.

Mongkok Computer Centre

Chic interior of Izzue store

6 Izzue
MAP E4 ■ 26 Sai Yeung Choi St South

High-end clothing chain for urban warriors and fashionistas in search of the perfect outfit for a night out.

7 Brighten Floriculture
MAP E4 ■ 28 Flower Market Rd

The porcelain and ceramic vases and wickerwork flower baskets are not likely to win awards for style or design, but the collection is impressive and the prices are reasonable.

8 Chan Chi Kee Cutlery
MAP M1 ■ 316–318 Shanghai St

Good-value, sturdy woks, steamers, choppers and pretty much everything else you might desire for the well-equipped kitchen.

9 Sandra's Pearls
MAP M1 ■ 447 Jade Market stall, Kansu St

Reliable one-stop shop in the jade market for pearls, beads and jewellery. Open between 11am and 4pm.

10 Sneaker Street
MAP E4 ■ Fa Yuen St

Sports enthusiasts will be in their element here. With a high concentration of sports shops, this is the place to be if you're seeking sports shoes, particularly rare or special editions.

Cheap Eats

1 Majesty Chinese Restaurant

MAP E4 ■ 3/F Wu Sang House,
655 Nathan Rd ■ 2397 3822 ■ $

This bright, informal restaurant
serves excellent and inexpensive
dim sum breakfasts and dinners.

2 Ramen Taifu

MAP E4 ■ 39 Fife St, Mong
Kok ■ 2487 4488 ■ $

Find yourself transported to the
back streets of Tokyo at Ramen
Taifu, known for the signature
flavourful broth and chewy noodles.

3 Yee Shun Milk Company

MAP N2 ■ 63 Pilkem St
■ 2730 2799 ■ $

Steamed milk puddings, flavoured
custards and other local sweets
abound at this popular restaurant.

4 Kedai Kopi Semua Semua

MAP E4 ■ Shop G01, G/F, 618 Shanghai
St, Mong Kok ■ 2389 3829 ■ $

Nasi lemak, beef rendang, pandan
cake: you'll find it all here at this
Malaysian café.

5 Saint's Alp Teahouse

MAP E4 ■ 5 Jordan Rd
■ 2374 0398 ■ No credit cards ■ $

Quirky snacks and an intriguing
menu of teas in a modern Taiwan-
style Chinese teahouse, which is
one of an extensive chain.

6 Tim Ho Wan

MAP E4 ■ G/F Olympian
City 2, 18 Hoi Ting Rd, Tai Kok Tsui
■ 2332 2896 ■ $

Large crowds queue up for the
Michelin-star-rated lotus-leaf rice
packets, *cha siu* (barbecued pork)

Diners at Tim Ho Wan

baked buns, persimmon cakes and
delicious *fun goh* (pork and shrimp)
dumplings served here.

7 Ah Long Pakistan Halal Food

MAP N2 ■ 95B Woosung St ■ 2782
1635 ■ No credit cards ■ $

Set amid busy surroundings near
Temple Street, this place is a good
bet if you fancy a decent spicy curry.

8 Veggie Family

MAP E4 ■ B/F, Ching Wah
Bldg, 145 Sai Yee St, Mong Kok
■ 2393 8012 ■ $

The friendly staff, generous helpings
and tasty veggie recipes attract not
just vegetarians but a wide clientele
to this restaurant.

9 Mr Wong's Restaurant

MAP E4 ■ 10 Shamchun St,
Mong Kok ■ 2384 6833 ■ $

This friendly restaurant, with its
cheap beers, is a hit among
university exchange students.

10 Light Vegetarian

MAP N2 ■ 13 Jordan Rd
■ 2384 2833 ■ $

There are Cantonese mock-meat
dishes on the à la carte menu, but
for the best deal, opt for the ample
lunchtime buffet, which includes
desserts and a pot of tea.

See map on p92

TOP 10 **New Kowloon**

New Kowloon was home to the international airport of Hong Kong, Kai Tak, from 1925 until 1998. The site has not been allowed to lie fallow, with the former terminal having been converted into the largest golf driving range in the world. Dotted around the neighbouring streets are excellent budget dining options and secondhand shops, for this is where the locals go bargain-hunting. Many cultural attractions can also be found to the north, in the Tang dynasty-style architecture of the Chi Lin Nunnery or in the joyful chaos of the Wong Tai Sin Temple.

Colourful Wong Tai Sin Temple

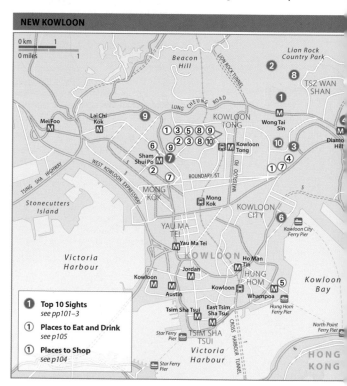

NEW KOWLOON

- ① Top 10 Sights
  see pp101–3
- ① Places to Eat and Drink
  see p105
- ① Places to Shop
  see p104

Previous pages Chinese lanterns and burning coils of incense inside Man Mo Temple

1 Wong Tai Sin Temple
MAP E4 ■ Chuk Un ■ 2327 8141 ■ Open 7am–5:30pm daily

A noisy, colourful affair, Wong Tai Sin Temple is always crowded and aswirl with incense smoke. Legend holds that Wong Tai Sin (originally known as Huang Chuping), who was born in Zhejiang province around AD 328, could see the future and make wishes come true. The temple opened in 1921, after a Taoist priest brought a sacred portrait of Huang to Hong Kong. The stylized architecture of the temple contrasts sharply with the surrounding concrete boxes. Worshippers from the three main Chinese religions – Confucianism, Taoism and Buddhism – flock here, not to mention tens of soothsayers hawking their services. Behind the temple is an ancient tomb that still baffles historians.

Lion Rock, resembling a lion's head

2 Lion Rock
MAP E4

One of the best places to view this fascinating landmark is, conveniently, from outside Wong Tai Sin temple. Find the open area near the fortune-tellers' stalls where you can look straight up at what, from this angle, resembles the head of a lion. Those feeling energetic may be tempted to scale its heights. Take lots of water, and be warned – the top section is not for the faint-hearted.

3 Kowloon Walled City Park
MAP E4

One of Hong Kong's most picturesque parks began life in 1847 as a Chinese fort. A legal oversight by the British left it under Chinese control after the New Territories were leased out to Britain. It was levelled during World War II, and a ghetto called the Walled City sprang up in its place. This bizarre place was a magnet for triads, drug dealers and heroin addicts (see p102). It was pulled down in 1992 and replaced by the park, which now features pretty gardens and preserved artifacts. A photography display in the almshouse illustrates its story.

Bonsai, Kowloon Walled City Park

Pagoda in Nan Lian Garden, opposite Chi Lin Nunnery

Chi Lin Nunnery

MAP F4 ■ Chi Lin Dr, Diamond Hill ■ Nunnery: 2354 1888; restaurant: 3658 9388 ■ Open 9am–4:30pm daily

It is said that not a single nail was used in the construction of this lavish replica of a Tang dynasty (AD 618–907) place of worship. The nunnery opened in 2000, funded by donations from wealthy families. The hall and side wings house impressive statues, including those of Sakyamuni Buddha and the Bodhisattva Guanyin. Opposite the nunnery lies the Nan Lian Garden, which was also designed on Tang dynasty principles. Artfully arranged rocks, trees, bridges and pavilions conceal its location in the middle of a busy traffic circle. Be sure to taste the food at the Chi Lin vegetarian restaurant located here, which is run by the nuns.

Lei Yue Mun

MAP F5

Once a fishing village, Lei Yue Mun translates as "carp gate", although the only fish you're likely to see nowadays are in the excellent seafood restaurants that line the waterfront. Lei Yue Mun is the closest point between Hong Kong Island and Kowloon, but don't be tempted to swim across the channel – you may get whisked away by the strong currents, so exercise caution and be responsible.

Cattle Depot Artist Village

MAP F4 ■ 63 Ma Tau Kok Rd, To Kwa Wan ■ 2364 2959 ■ Open 10am–10pm daily

Originally a slaughterhouse, this old, red brick building was renovated in 2001 and developed into a creative hub for artists. Enjoy the quirky galleries, exhibitions and art park here.

⑦ Apliu Street Flea Market

MAP E4 ■ Apliu St ■ Open 9am–5pm daily

This huge street market (see p56) is full of all sorts of odd knick-knacks and pirated goods at cut-throat prices. Some of the items, like old school mobile phones or a retro turntable or radio, are from another era. It includes perhaps the world's biggest collection of secondhand electrical appliances.

THE MOST DENSELY POPULATED PLACE ON THE PLANET

More than 50,000 people once inhabited the Kowloon Walled City (see p101), a place of few laws, but plenty of disease and criminality. In the 1950s the Triads moved in and governed in their own ruthless style. Before 1992 it was one of the few places left in Hong Kong with opium addicts puffing away on divans.

⑧ Fat Jong Temple
MAP E4 ■ 171–175 Sha Tin Pass Rd, Wong Tai Sin ■ Open 9am–4pm Mon–Sun

Although it is one of the most famous Buddhist sites in Hong Kong, Fat Jong Temple is little-visited by foreigners. Making it well worth the journey to see are the striking colour scheme (with red pillars standing out from the white walls), ornate decorations and magnificent Buddha sculptures. The temple somehow manages to be busy and serene at the same time.

⑨ Lei Cheng Uk Tomb
MAP E4 ■ 41 Tonkin St, Sham Shui Po ■ 2386 2863 ■ Open 10am–6pm Fri–Wed

The Han burial tomb (AD 24–220) can barely be seen through a scratched sheet of Perspex. Still, it's one of Hong Kong's earliest surviving historical monuments housed within its own museum, so act suitably impressed.

⑩ Hau Wong Temple
MAP E4 ■ Junction Rd ■ 2336 0375 ■ Open 8am–5pm daily

Quaint and tiny, Hau Wong Temple is hardly worth a special trip, but take a look if you're in the area. It was built in the 1730s, however there seem to be a number of legends surrounding its origins. It's usually fairly quiet unless a festival is in full swing.

Entrance to tiny Hau Wong Temple

AN AFTERNOON IN NEW KOWLOON

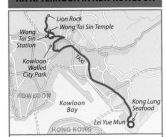

▶ **AFTER LUNCH**

Catch the MTR to Wong Tai Sin Station and brave the crowds of earnest worshippers at **Wong Tai Sin Temple** *(see p101)*. Some of the fortune-tellers in the nearby stalls speak English. It's easy to bargain them down to a third or quarter of the price given. Some use numbered sticks, while others prefer curved bits of wood known as Buddha's lips.

If you're feeling fit, tackle **Lion Rock** *(see p101)*. It's a demanding climb, but the views are superb. The steep inclines towards the top are for the stout of heart only. Take plenty of water.

A 10-minute taxi ride will take you to the **Kowloon Walled City Park** *(see p101)*, Hong Kong's loveliest urban park. This tranquil green space contains eight different gardens.

LATE AFTERNOON

By late afternoon you should have worked up an appetite, so take a cab to the seafood restaurants on the waterfront at **Lei Yue Mun**. Watch the sun paint the skyscrapers pink and orange as it sinks into the harbour, while you crack open crabs and munch on giant shrimps, all washed down with wine or an icy Tsing Tao beer.

With huge stone lions guarding its front door, one restaurant that is difficult to miss in Lei Yue Mun is **Kong Lung Seafood** *(see p105)*. Here you can feast on a range of tasty dishes, including deep-roasted crab and steamed abalone with orange crust.

See map on pp100–101

Places to Shop

1 Bookazine
MAP E4 ▪ Shop UG46, Festival Walk, Kowloon Tong

A massive branch of Hong Kong's great bookshop chain, this gets top marks for all the bestseller novels, latest international magazines as well as a selection of greeting cards.

2 Dragon Centre
MAP E4 ▪ 37K Yen Chou St, cnr Cheung Sha Wan Rd, Sham Shui Po

Soaring glassy mall in the midst of Sham Shui Po's underbelly. Good food hall, computer tech and even an ice rink.

3 i.t.
MAP E4 ▪ Shop LG2–02, Festival Walk, Kowloon Tong

This smart, minimalist outlet stocks stylish Japanese and American street clothes and accessories.

4 Yuet Tung China Works
MAP F4 ▪ 3/F Kowloon Bay Industrial Centre, 15 Wang Hoi Rd, Kowloon Bay

One of the last places in Hong Kong still making Cantonese ceramics – tableware, decorative, personalized or monogrammed. Orders may take four weeks but shipping can be arranged.

5 Lancôme
MAP E4 ▪ G18 Festival Walk, Kowloon Tong ▪ 2265 8665

Ubiquitous luxury French cosmetics brand. Take your pick from the skin check-up or the 45-minute VIP consultation, or go straight for a beauty treatment in a private cabin.

Lancôme storefront display

6 Golden Computer Arcade
MAP E4 ▪ 146–152 Fuk Wa St, Sham Shui Po

Spread across four chaotic floors is computer equipment available at good prices. Take care – many of the PS4 games and manga figurines available here are knock-offs.

Inside the Golden Computer Arcade

7 Yu Chau Street and Nam Cheong Street
MAP E4

The small shops that line these two streets sell laces, zippers, ribbons, and buttons – a wider choice than you might have imagined could exist.

8 BEYORG Beyond Organic
MAP E4 ▪ Shop UG17, Festival Walk, Kowloon Tong

Organic, sweet-smelling goodies to pamper yourself with here. One of a number of branches across town.

9 COVA Cake-Chocolate Shop
MAP E4 ▪ Shop LG1–10 Festival Walk, Kowloon Tong ▪ 2265 8678 ▪ $

Relish the taste of sumptuous high-end cakes, confectionery and chocolates that are flown in daily from Milan.

10 Millies
MAP F4 ▪ Shop F26, 1/F Telford Plaza I, Kowloon Bay ▪ 2673 2780

One of the Hong Kong outlets of the largest retailer of women's shoes in China. It stocks a great range of shoes, particularly its own label.

Places to Eat and Drink

PRICE CATEGORIES

For a three-course meal for one with half a bottle of wine and extra charges. Prices are quoted in Hong Kong dollars.

$ under $250 $$ $250–600 $$$ over $600

1 Cambo Thai
MAP E4 ■ 25 Nga Tsin Long Rd, Kowloon City ■ 2716 7318 ■ $$
Kowloon City is famous for its cheap and tasty Thai food. Be warned that you may need a cold beer to accompany the spicy beef salad.

2 TeaWood
MAP E4 ■ Shop G11, Festival Walk, Kowloon Tong ■ 2336 0277 ■ $
This forest-themed café serves Taiwanese-style snacks and a wide selection of teas and coffees.

3 Exp
MAP E4 ■ Shop UG23, Festival Walk, Kowloon Tong ■ 2265 8298 ■ $
A well-priced option serving Western and Asian favourites. Specializing in pizza, spaghetti and noodles, all with an interesting twist.

4 Chong Fat Chiu Chow Restaurant
MAP E4 ■ 60–62 South Wall Rd, Kowloon City ■ 2383 3114 ■ $
If you want to try traditional Chiu Chow seafood, this restaurant serves some of the best. Go for the tasty crab or goose dishes.

5 Wing Lai Yuen Sichuan Noodles
MAP F4 ■ 15–17 Fung Tak Rd ■ 2726 3818 ■ $
Traditional Szechuan food in a plain setting. The dan dan noodles are the most delicious thing on the menu.

6 Kong Lung Seafood
MAP F4 ■ 62 Hoi Pong Rd W, Lei Yue Mun ■ 2775 1552 ■ $$
You can't miss this place – two huge stone lions guard the front door. This is a good bet for decent, fresh seafood. The deep-roasted crab and the steamed abalone with citrus reticulata rate highly.

7 Tso Choi Koon
MAP E4 ■ 17–19A Nga Tsin Wai Rd, Kowloon City ■ 2383 7170 ■ No credit cards ■ $
With a name that translates to "rough food", this is one for those prepared to take some culinary risks to experience the real Hong Kong. The adventurous dishes include sautéed pig's intestines and fried pig's brains.

8 Bloom by Wang Jia Sha
MAP E4 ■ Shop G23, Festival Walk, Kowloon Tong ■ 2265 8488 ■ $$
This small chain offers an extensive range of dim sum. The chefs, brought in from the mainland, produce their own Shanghai-style take on them.

9 Kung Wo Beancurd Factory
MAP E4 ■ 118 Pei Ho St, Sham Shui Po ■ 2386 6871 ■ $
This humble spot specializes in all things tofu. Wash the deep fried tofu down with homemade soya bean milk.

10 Amaroni's
MAP E4 ■ Shop LG1-32 Festival Walk, Kowloon Tong ■ 2265 8818 ■ $
Hong Kongers love Italian, and they have taken this place to their heart. Share the classic Italian dishes and make yourself at home.

Cosy setting of Amaroni's

See map on pp100–101

TOP 10 The New Territories

As a name, the New Territories is quite suggestive of frontier country – and in colonial times this was indeed the place where pith-helmeted sahibs went on tiger shoots, threw tennis parties and wrote memoirs. Today, much of the region is suburban rather than rural: more than a third of the population of Hong Kong lives here, in dormitory towns dotted across "the NT", as it is abbreviated by the locals. But to the north are the largest expanses of open country to be found in Hong Kong, including the important Mai Po Nature Reserve, and there are centuries-old temples and settlements here, too. At the northern extremity of the New Territories is the border with "mainland" China.

Pagoda, Ten Thousand Buddhas Monastery

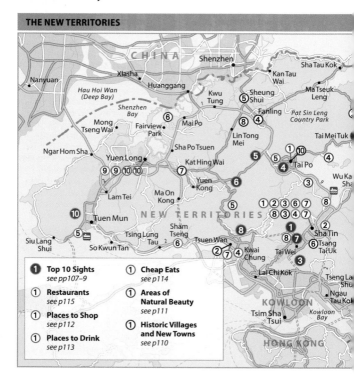

THE NEW TERRITORIES

1 Top 10 Sights *see pp107–9*	**1** Cheap Eats *see p114*
1 Restaurants *see p115*	**1** Areas of Natural Beauty *see p111*
1 Places to Shop *see p112*	**1** Historic Villages and New Towns *see p110*
1 Places to Drink *see p113*	

1 Ten Thousand Buddhas Monastery

MAP E3 ■ East Rail Line to Sha Tin, take exit B and follow signs ■ 2691 1067 ■ Open 9am–5:30pm daily

The Buddhas in question are stacked on shelves in the main hall of this hillside sanctuary at Pai Tau Tsuen, Sha Tin. In fact, there are more like 12,000 Buddha images now. The monastery comprises five temples, two pavilions and an elegant nine-storey pagoda. Take a deep breath before you enter the grounds – there are 400-odd steps to negotiate.

2 Tai Wai to Tai Mei Tuk Cycling Trail

MAP F2

The cycling route from Tai Wai to Tai Mei Tuk route is one of Hong Kong's most scenic trails. Rent a bike in Tai Wai and cycle along the Shing Mun River, making a stop at the Science

Park for lunch before continuing on your way. The trail tends to be crowded at the weekends, especially with families and young children, so cycle this route on a weekday if possible. When you arrive at Tai Mei Tuk, reward yourself at one of the neighbourhood cafés and take a moment to admire the Plover Cove Reservoir. You can return your bike at the shops here and catch public transport back to town.

Embankment in Plover Cove Reservoir

3 Amah Rock

MAP E4 ■ East Rail Line to Tai Wai

This odd tower of rocks near Lion Rock Tunnel, when viewed from a certain angle, looks eerily like a woman with a baby on her back – hence the name. Legend holds that the amah's husband sailed overseas to find work, while she patiently waited for his return. When a storm sank his boat, she was so grief-stricken she turned to stone. An alternative interpretation is that the rock was created as an ancient phallic symbol.

Amah Rock

4 Hong Kong Railway Museum

MAP E2 ▪ 13 Shung Tak St, Tai Po ▪ 2653 3455 ▪ East Rail Line to Tai Po Market, then follow signs ▪ Open 10am–6pm Mon & Wed–Sun ▪ www.heritagemuseum.gov.hk

This museum is a prime attraction for trainspotters. Old coaches sit on tracks outside what used to be Tai Po Market Station. Inside is a tolerably interesting account of the city. Guided tours are also available.

Wishes on Lam Tsuen Wishing Trees

5 Lam Tsuen Wishing Trees

MAP E2 ▪ Lam Tsuen Village ▪ MTR to Tai Po Market, then Bus 64K or 64P to Fong Ma Po Station

People used to throw wishes, written on weighted strips of paper, from the branches of these trees on holy days. The practice was banned after the overloaded limbs broke off, so now wishes are pinned on a nearby board.

6 Kadoorie Farm

MAP E2 ▪ Lam Kam Rd, Tai Po ▪ 2483 7200 ▪ Bus 64K from Tai Po Market East Rail Line ▪ Open 9:30am–5pm daily (last adm 4pm) ▪ Adm ▪ www.kfbg.org.hk

Set up by local moguls Sir Horace Kadoorie and Lord Lawrence in 1951 to provide work for some 300,000 penniless refugees, Kadoorie Farm and Botanic Garden is now a centre for conservation and environmental awareness, promoting biodiversity in Hong Kong. Today, its 148 hectares (365 acres) of land include a deer haven and butterfly house.

7 Heritage Museum

Sha Tin's Heritage Museum (see pp26–7) vies with the revamped Museum of History in Kowloon for the title of Hong Kong's top museum.

8 Yuen Yuen Institute

MAP E3 ▪ 2492 2220 ▪ MTR to Tsuen Wan, then minibus 81 ▪ Open 8:30am–5pm daily

This temple complex is popular with Buddhists, Confucianists and Taoists alike. It's usually full of worshippers, so be respectful. The main building is a replica of Beijing's Temple of Heaven. The notices outside carry the latest soothsayers' wisdom on which signs in the Chinese horoscope are set for an auspicious year. Try the tasty vegetarian food in the Institute's restaurant.

Yuen Yuen Institute

SAVING THE SANCTUARY

The New Territories' Mai Po Nature Reserve *(see p44)* is a world-class site of ecological significance, with more than 90,000 birds stopping there on migratory routes each winter. Kingfishers, herons and cormorants abound, and the marsh is one of the last habitats for the near-extinct black-faced spoonbill and Saunders' gull **(below)**. Hong Kong's premier birdwatchers' paradise has been the subject of fierce debate and hard-fought battles between staunch environmentalists and developers desperate for scarce new land. The environmentalists, fortunately, have the upper hand. The biggest danger is pollution and industrial waste seeping into the marsh from factories at nearby Deep Water Bay.

9 Tin Hau Temple at Lam Tsuen

MAP G5 ■ 2638 3678 ■ MTR to Tai Po Market, then Bus 64K or 64P to Fong Ma Po Station ■ Open 8am–5pm daily

At the far end of Clearwater Bay sits the oldest of Hong Kong's temples dedicated to the sea goddess Tin Hau. The descent to it through a patch of forest is eerily quiet. Inside, spirals of incense drop ash onto models of fishing boats.

10 Tsing Shan Monastery

MAP B3 ■ Castle Peak, Tuen Mun ■ 2441 6666 ■ West Rail Line to Tuen Mun ■ Open 6am–6pm daily

The 2-km (1-mile) walk from the railway station is hard, but this is a pleasant outing to relieve stress if the city's bustle is getting to you. Soak up some fresh sea air and let the chanting of the monks soothe your soul.

A DAY IN THE NEW TERRITORIES

▶ MORNING

Take the MTR to Kowloon Tong Station, then switch to the East Rail Line. Get off at Tai Po Market station, and take the 64K or 64P bus or a taxi to Lam Tsuen, home to the **Lam Tsuen Wishing Trees**. Buy a red paper strip from nearby stalls, pen down your wish, then affix it to the adjacent boards.

Head back to the East Rail Line, and proceed to Fanling Station. Take the 54K bus to Lung Yeuk Tau, start of the **Lung Yeuk Tau Heritage Trail** *(see p110)*. This path takes you through the five famous walled villages of the New Territories, which were built by ancient clans as safe havens from bandits. The walk takes a couple of hours, and provides a fascinating insight into what life once was like in these parts.

AFTERNOON

Take a bus or taxi back to the East Rail Line, and travel on to Sha Tin Station. A short cab ride away is the **Lung Wah Hotel** *(22 Ha Wo Che St; 2691 1594)*, which isn't a hotel any more, but a restaurant. This eating house, with a sea of iconic red lanterns at its entrance, has been going strong for more than 50 years.

If you are in Tai Wai *(see p110)* during a cooler month, consider a leisurely bike ride along the Shing Mun River.

On weekdays or when the weather is not so forgiving, check out the chic shops at **New Town Plaza** *(see p112)*.

See map on pp106–7 ←

Historic Villages and New Towns

Market stalls, selling fish straight off the boat, line the waterfront at Sai Kung

1 Sai Kung
MAP F3

Quaint fishing village turned expatriate haunt. Pubs with names such as The Boozer and the Duke of York are offset by old Chinese men playing mahjong in tiny cafés.

2 Tsuen Wan
MAP D3

This is the terminus of the MTR line. The district is home to the office complex, Nina Tower, one of Hong Kong's tallest buildings.

3 Sha Tin
MAP E3

A residential district, with a massive shopping centre, Sha Tin is also home to Hong Kong's second racetrack.

4 Fanling
MAP E2

Fanling's 16th-century Tang Chung Ling ancestral hall belongs to the foremost clan in the New Territories. The Lung Yeuk Tau Heritage Trail is located nearby.

5 Sheung Shui
MAP E1

Home to one of the New Territories' local clans, the Liu. Situated nearby is Lok Ma Chau, a border crossing with China, where the towering skyline of Shenzhen looms through the smog. There's also an ancestral hall here.

6 Tsang Tai Uk
MAP F3 ■ Near Lion Rock Tunnel Rd, Sha Tin Wai

This stronghold (see p47) of the Tsang clan dates back to 1848 and is built in typical Hakka style, with thick walls and a defensive tower in each corner.

7 Kam Tin
MAP C3

The name of this town means "brocade field", fitting for its sprawling farms still churning out produce today. Nearby are two traditional walled villages, Kat Hing Wai and Shui Tau.

8 Ping Kong
MAP E1

Off the beaten track, and therefore its walled village is less busy than others. The tiny Tin Hau Temple was featured in Jackie Chan's cult martial arts comedy Project A.

9 Tap Mun Chau
MAP H2 ■ Ferries: from Ma Liu Shui daily; www.tsuiwahferry.com

One of the New Territories' best-kept secrets, this is a picturesque little island where villagers watch the world go by from their quaint homes.

10 Tai Po
MAP E2

Its market and Railway Museum (see p108) are worth a quick look, before heading to scenic Plover Cove.

Areas of Natural Beauty

1 Plover Cove
MAP F2

This isn't actually a cove, at least, not any more. In fact it's a massive reservoir that was created by building a dam across the mouth of the bay, then pumping all the seawater out and pumping in fresh water from China. Hike or bike the trails. Maps from HKTB.

Idyllic Plover Cove

2 Bride's Pool
MAP F2

Stunning waterfalls plunge into the pool amid the forest *(see p44)*. Take a camera and wear sensible shoes.

3 Tai Po Kau
MAP F2

This forest reserve near the Chinese University is popular with avid bird-watchers and hikers. Be wary of the monkeys while visiting Tai Po Kau.

4 Sam Mun Tsai
MAP F2

A charming fishing village perched between verdant hills and sparkling Plover Cove. Check out the local fisherfolks' charming floating homes.

5 Tai Mo Shan
MAP E3

"Big fog-shrouded mountain" is the translation, although on many days the peak of Hong Kong's tallest mountain is visible. It reaches 957 m (3,139 ft) – quite a hike to the top, but superb views await the intrepid.

6 Mai Po Nature Reserve
MAP D2 ■ www.wwf.org.hk

The marsh *(see p44)* on the western edge of the New Territories is a bird sanctuary and nature reserve.

7 Clearwater Bay
MAP G5

Various walks and beaches are on offer here. From Tai Au Mun, you can walk to the less than inspiringly named Clearwater Bay Beach One and Beach Two or Lung Ha Wan (Lobster Bay). There are occasional shark sightings during the summer, so beware before taking a swim.

8 Long Ke Wan
MAP H3

Relatively inaccessible little gem of a beach. Don't get too carried away with the view as you descend the vertiginous goat track, or you may find yourself at the bottom sooner than you intended.

9 Ma On Shan
MAP F3

The mountain's name means "saddle", a reference to its shape *(see p45)*. Popular with hikers.

10 Tai Long Wan
MAP H3

Hong Kong's finest beach *(see pp28–9)*, on the beautiful Sai Kung Peninsula. Take a good map and lots of water before setting off.

Turquoise waters of Tai Long Wan

See map on pp106–7

Places to Shop

1 IKEA
MAP F3 ▪ L6 HomeSquare, 138 Sha Tin Rural Committee Rd, Sha Tin

Even those who are not normally fans of the Swedish chain will find the wide array of made-in-China goods attractive.

2 Citylink Plaza
MAP E3 ▪ Sha Tin Station

This mall offers a wider range of more affordable brands than the nearby New Town Plaza.

3 New Town Plaza
MAP E3 ▪ 18–19 Sha Tin Centre St, Sha Tin

This is the place to come to in Sha Tin for designer brands and high-end shopping. There are also cinemas and plenty of restaurants and a rose garden. An added attraction is Snoopy's World for children, a small outdoor theme park featuring all the *Peanuts* characters.

4 Overjoy Porcelain Factory
MAP D3 ▪ 1/F Block B, Kwai Hing Industrial Bldg, 10 Chun Pin St, Kwai Chung ▪ 2487 0615

There are hundreds of patterns on offer, making this the perfect place to buy your dinner service.

5 Tai Po's Produce Markets
MAP E2 ▪ East Rail Line to Tai Po Market Station, then follow signs to temple

Tai Po is packed with atmospheric markets; those outside Fu Shin Street's Man Mo Temple are the best.

6 UNIQLO
MAP E3 ▪ Shop 225, 2/F New Town Plaza, Sha Tin

High-quality, but affordable Japanese clothing store. It has 18 branches all over Hong Kong.

Shoppers at the UNIQLO store

7 Marks & Spencer
MAP E3 ▪ A331, Level 3, New Town Plaza 3, Sha Tin

Sensible shoes as well as comfortable casual and formalwear are available at this popular British chain.

8 Muji
MAP E3 ▪ A221, Level 2, New Town Plaza 3, Sha Tin

Big branch of the Japanese chain store. Stock up on comfy cotton clothing and household goods here.

9 Hang Heung Bakery
MAP C2 ▪ 66 Castle Peak Rd, Yuen Long ▪ 2474 5731

Hong Kong's most popular baker of "wife cakes", a flaky pastry filled with red-bean paste. These traditional confections are *de rigueur* at Chinese wedding ceremonies.

10 Wing Wah Bakery
MAP C2 ▪ 4–6 On Ning Rd, Yuen Long ▪ 2476 9966

The city's premier purveyor of moon cakes *(see p52)*, these rich pastry treats are eaten during the Mid-Autumn festival. The egg yolks in the centre represent the full moon, although other fillings are available.

Stall at Tai Po's Produce Markets

Places to Drink

1 After 5
MAP E2 ▪ Shop A, 5 Mei Sun Ln, Tai Po ▪ 2663 3551

The most popular of Tai Po's few Western-style bars, with cold beers from around the world. Steer clear of the overpriced wine list. There's also a pool table here.

2 Golem Craft Beer
MAP E3 ▪ Shop G07, G/F, Kings Wings Plaza 2, 1 On Kwan St, Shek Mun, Sha Tin ▪ 2350 9116

Craft beer fans will be spoiled for choice at this bar tucked away in a shopping mall. It offers a variety of local beers on tap.

3 The Picture House
MAP F3 ▪ 66 Yi Chun St, Sai Kung ▪ 2792 6991

This little place serves wines and cocktails, along with flat breads, salads and Western-style snacks.

4 Poets
MAP F3 ▪ G/F 55 Yi Chun St, Sai Kung ▪ 2791 7993

Don't let the name fool you. Loud discussions about the previous night's Premier League football matches are more likely than pompous declamations in iambic pentameter at this British-style pub.

5 The Boozer
MAP F3 ▪ 57 Yi Chun St, Sai Kung ▪ 2792 9311

Much of Sai Kung's expatriate population can be found playing darts or watching sport on flat-screen TVs, while eating food brought in from the numerous neighbouring restaurants.

6 Bacco
MAP F3 ▪ 21 Man Nin St, Sai Kung ▪ 2574 7477

For a more sophisticated experience head to Bacco, where you can sample their extensive list of wines by the bottle or the glass. Upstairs is JoJo, an Indian restaurant run by the same management team.

7 Regal Riverside Hotel
MAP E3 ▪ 34–36 Tai Chung Kiu Rd, Sha Tin ▪ 2649 7878

Three bars are on offer at this monolithic hotel – one lively and sports-oriented, the others more casual with great cocktail menus. All offer a respite from a hard day's shopping in New Town Plaza.

8 Tikitiki Bowling Bar
MAP F3 ▪ 4/F, Centro, 1A Chui Tong Rd, Sai Kung ▪ 2657 8488

This is a perfect place for a family outing. The decor is stylish and it features a restaurant, two bars and ten bowling lanes. There's also a DJ, and live bands perform too.

Chic interiors of Padstow

9 Padstow
MAP F3 ▪ 112 Pak Sha Wan, Sai Kung ▪ 2335 5515

There is a lovely colonial feel to this two-storied, balconied building, painted sky blue. Upstairs, the sea-view tables offer a perfect spot to enjoy a drink. This place is ideal for weekend brunches.

10 Duke of York
MAP F3 ▪ 42–56 Fuk Man Rd, Sai Kung ▪ 2792 8435

This old school British-style pub in Sai Kung enjoys a loyal following. The friendly staff here serves a wide selection of beers amid a relaxed setting.

See map on pp106–7

Cheap Eats

Table setting at Pepperoni's

① Pepperoni's
MAP F3 ■ 1592 Po Tung Rd, Sai Kung ■ 2791 1738 ■ $$

One of the first decent Western-style restaurants in Sai Kung, Pepperoni's has a relaxed ambience. Offers pizza, pasta, nachos, calamari alongside a good wine selection.

② New Tak Kee Seafood Restaurant
MAP F3 ■ 55 See Cheung St, Sai Kung ■ 2792 0006 ■ $$

Buy your seafood from the market opposite or straight from the boats at the dock and this one-of-a-kind restaurant will cook it in your choice of Cantonese style.

③ Lardos Steak House
MAP F4 ■ G/F 4B Hang Hau Village, Tseung Kwan O, Sai Kung ■ 2719 8168 ■ $$

Steaks are cooked to perfection by an owner who supplies Hong Kong's best hotels with their meat. The set lunch menu is popular.

④ Ali-Oli Bakery Café
MAP F3 ■ 11 Sha Tsui Path, Sai Kung ■ 2792 2655 ■ $

This bakery serves big breakfasts and pasta dishes, as well as the usual café fare, including delicious sandwiches and croissants.

⑤ Fuk Man Road
MAP F3 ■ Sai Kung ■ $

This road runs from the centre of town to the bus stations and is lined with noodle restaurants for the locals; dishes are usually served with brisket or offal so be careful what you order.

⑥ Yau Ley
MAP H4 ■ High Island, Sai Kung ■ No credit cards ■ 2791 1822 (booking rec) ■ $$ (set menu only)

Fabulous seafood set menus in a little restaurant nestling in Sha Kiu village, reachable by road, hiking, ferry or the restaurant's boat.

⑦ Simplicity
MAP D3 ■ 3/F Kowloon Panda Hotel, 3 Tsuen Wah St, Tsuen Wan ■ 2409 3226 ■ $$

Dig into a good-value buffet or load up on cut-price pasta from the set menus offered here.

⑧ Hao Tang Hao Mian
MAP E3 ■ 20 Chik Chueng St, Tai Wai ■ 2813 5077 ■ $

This restaurant serves soupy noodles with premium ingredients like Wagyu beef cheek and ox tongue.

⑨ Honeymoon Dessert
MAP F3 ■ 9–10D Po Tung Rd, Sai Kung ■ 2792 4991 ■ $

Good-sized portions of various traditional desserts, with durian eaters segregated so as not to offend others with the strong smell of the fruit. Open until late.

⑩ Shaffi's Indian
MAP C2 ■ Fook Tak Bldg, 234 Castle Peak Rd ■ 2476 7885 ■ $

This long-standing Indian diner is considered a Hong Kong institution. Founded in 1972, the restaurant would serve curries to the British soldiers at their Shek Kong base. It offers tasty and affordable lunch-time set menus.

Restaurants

PRICE CATEGORIES

For a three-course meal for one with half a bottle of wine (or equivalent meal) and extra charges.

$ under $250 **$$** $250–600 **$$$** over $600

1 Jaspas
MAP F3 ■ 13 Sha Tsui Path, Sai Kung ■ 2792 6388 ■ $$

Part of a chain, Jaspas has good fusion food, friendly staff and antipodean wines at reasonable prices.

2 Tung Kee Seafood Restaurant
MAP F3 ■ 9/F, 96–102 Man Nin St, Sai Kung ■ 2791 9886 ■ $$

Point at what you want from the huge range of sea creatures swimming in waterfront tanks and haggle a bit. They bag it and cook it for you. One of the best seafood meals in Hong Kong.

3 Loaf On
MAP F3 ■ 49 See Cheung St, Sai Kung ■ 2792 9966 ■ $$$

Sai Kung's first Michelin-starred restaurant, Loaf On serves delicious Cantonese cuisine. Some locals claim the seafood dishes are the equal of any Hong Kong restaurant.

4 Jade Pavilion
MAP E3 ■ 2/F Royal Park Hotel, 8 Pak Hok Ting St, Sha Tin ■ 2694 3939 ■ $$

Classy Cantonese cooking – not an easy thing to find in Sha Tin. Specialities include dim sum, seafood and crispy chicken.

5 Tao Heung
MAP C3 ■ S40–S44, Ocean Walk, Tuen Mun ■ 8300 8135 ■ $

Bright, noisy dim sum restaurant in Tai Po, Tao Heung serves all the favourites: *har gau* prawn dumplings, *cheung fun* rice rolls and crispy *cha siu* pastries.

6 Yue Kee Roasted Goose Restaurant
MAP D3 ■ 9 Sham Tseng San Tsuen, Sham Tseng ■ 2491 0105 ■ $$

Stewed goose innards are the best part of the meal here for many local customers, but its strong flavours might not be for everyone.

7 The Terrace
MAP F3 ■ 168 Che Keng Tuk Rd, Sai Kung ■ 2792 1436 ■ $$

A child-friendly restaurant that serves good Italian food. Its terrace, after which it is named, offers a lovely view over the marina.

8 Sha Tin 18
MAP E3 ■ 18 Chak Cheung St, Sha Tin ■ 3723 1234 ■ $$

In the Sha Tin Hyatt Regency Hotel, this chic Chinese restaurant with an outdoor terrace is great for southern Chinese seafood and meat dishes.

9 Tai Wing Wah
MAP C2 ■ 2–6 On Ning Rd, Yuen Long ■ 2476 9888 ■ $

Specializes in dim sum brunches and Poon Choi – a traditional New Territories casserole.

10 One Thirty-One
MAP F3 ■ 131 Tseng Tsau Village, Shap Sze Heung, Sai Kung ■ 2791 2684 ■ Closed Mon, Tue–Fri L ■ $$$

Accessible by road or private boat, this place serves fixed menus from its own organic farm. Book ahead.

One Thirty-One

See map on pp106–7 ←

TOP 10 Outlying Islands

Hong Kong is often perceived as a city rather than an archipelago, but there are 260 islands in the group and, assuming you can haul yourself out of the bars and boutiques in downtown, some of the territory's most sublime experiences await you here. Now that it's connected to the city by bridge, the largest of the islands, Lantau, is losing the quirky languor it once had, but the smaller islands offer plenty of compensation. From the narrow lanes of Cheung Chau to the outdoor raves of Lamma's Power Station Beach, Hong Kong's many islands give you ample opportunity to relax and unwind.

Mui Wo beach, Lantau

① Lantau: Mui Wo
MAP C5 ■ Ferries from Hong Kong Island

Silvermine Bay, as the British named Mui Wo, is a good starting point from which to explore Lantau, though not the island's most beautiful spot. Most of the restaurants and bars, plus a supermarket, are around the corner from the ferry pier. There is also a beach 5 minutes' walk away. Enjoy a beer or stock up for a picnic before walking, cycling or beachcombing.

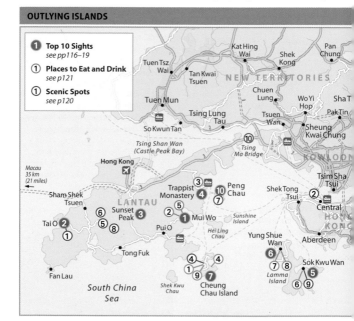

OUTLYING ISLANDS

① **Top 10 Sights**
see pp116–19

① **Places to Eat and Drink**
see p121

① **Scenic Spots**
see p120

Macau
35 km
(21 miles)

2 Lantau: Tai O
MAP A5

Lying on the far western coast of Lantau, the pretty village of Tai O is worth the long haul from downtown Hong Kong. Sitting in a tidal estuary, this is one of the last places in Hong Kong where you can still see the traditional stilt housing of southern Chinese fishing villages. Some are as small as dolls' houses. For Hong Kong consumable, buy a jar of shrimp paste, a powerful type of fish sauce made by fermenting shrimp and spices in a barrel in the sun. The delicious condiment is perfect with almost any dish.

3 Lantau: Sunset Peak
MAP B5

For the reasonably fit, Sunset Peak offers the finest views on Lantau. The 934-m (3,063-ft) high mountain, Hong Kong's second highest, commands great views across the region, down on the airport, along the new bridge to Po Lin Monastery and the lovely wooded valleys of this sparsely

The view from Sunset Peak, Lantau

inhabited terrain. Hardy souls stay at the nearby Youth Hostel and head up the peak for Hong Kong's most spectacular sunrise. Obviously all this only applies in clear conditions.

4 Lantau: Trappist Monastery
MAP C5

The chapel, next to a dilapidated old dairy farm, is open to visitors willing to observe the silence of the monastery. Apart from that, there is not much to see at the monastery itself, but it's a good excuse for a gentle woodland walk to or from Discovery Bay. The monastery is also served by a ferry pier, with infrequent *kaito* (small ferry) services to Discovery Bay and the island of Peng Chau (see p119), which has a number of good seafood restaurants.

Discovery Bay on Lantau

Seafood in Sok Kwu Wan

⑤ Lamma: Sok Kwu Wan

MAP E6 ■ Hong Kong Central
Pier 4 ■ www.hkkf.com.hk

Don't expect many sights in Lamma's main area of development on the east coast of the island. Sok Kwu Wan is known mainly for its quarry and the wall-to-wall seafood restaurants along its harbour front. The seafood tanks are a sight in themselves, however, with some monster-sized fish and crustaceans. There's not much to differentiate the restaurants here, although the standard is generally very good. Have a look at the pretty Tin Hau Temple at the end of the main street. The lovely 5-km (3-mile) circular walk to the sleepy, remote village and beach at Yung Shue Ha is recommended for the reasonably fit.

⑥ Lamma: Yung Shue Wan

MAP D5 ■ Regular ferries from Hong Kong Central Pier 4 ■ www. hkkf.com.hk

The western coast of Lamma also has a harbour, with lots of bars and eating choices along the endearingly

LANTAU'S PINK DOLPHINS

The endangered dolphins **(below)** of the Pearl River Delta can usually be found at play near the coast of Lantau. A guided boat trip to see them is certainly worthwhile. Learn about the lives of these creatures and the threats they face, including pollution, overfishing and lethal boat propellers and hydrofoils. Tours leave at least four times a week *(see p49)*.

ramshackle main street of the village. Watch villagers, resident expats and fellow visitors wander by, before hitting the well-kept beach at Hung Shing Ye, which is a 20-minute walk to the southwest.

⑦ Cheung Chau Island

This former pirate haven *(see pp30–31)* retains much of its traditional character, from the small-scale shipyards at the harbour's edge to the old temples and shrines that dot its narrow alleys. With many of its inhabitants still being fishermen, it's a good destination for seeking out some cheap seafood. There are also a couple of excellent beaches here.

Cheung Chau's pristine coastline backed by verdant hills

8 Tap Mun
MAP H2 ■ Ferries from Wong Shek and Ma Liu Shui ■ www.tsui wahferry.com

Lying north of the Sai Kung Peninsula, tiny Tap Mun, also known as "grass island", is another remote destination with only a couple of daily connections with the mainland. The rewards are striking rock formations, pounding seas, the striking Tin Hau Temple and relative seclusion. Take a picnic, as there are few eating opportunities. Nor is there any accommodation on the island, so be sure that you don't miss the last ferry back.

A rock formation on Po Toi

9 Po Toi
MAP F6 ■ Ferry from Stanley or Aberdeen Tue, Thu, Sat, Sun & public hols ■ www.tsuiwahferry.com

Getting to this barely inhabited outcrop of rock south of Hong Kong Island is most easily accomplished by taking the small "kaito" ferries that run from Stanley and Aberdeen. It's worth the effort for the secluded walks and spectacular cliff views over the South China Sea. Round off your day with a hearty meal at the island's only restaurant, Ming Kee Seafood (see p121).

10 Peng Chau
MAP C5 ■ Ferries from Hong Kong Central Pier 6 ■ www.hkkf. com.hk

This tiny island remains in many ways a traditional coastal community. You wander among its narrow alleys, tiny shops and temples to the tune of a game of mahjong or Cantonese opera leaking from an old radio. However, there's no beach, and very few eating choices, though the seafood is cheap.

A DAY ON LANTAU

▶ MORNING

Make a reasonably early start for Lantau from the outlying islands ferry terminal on Hong Kong Island. After disembarking at **Mui Wo** (see p116), take the No.1 bus from outside the ferry pier to the old fishing village of **Tai O** (see p117) located on the far north-western coast.

Take in the sights and smells of this ancient settlement before catching the No. 21 bus to Ngong Ping for the **Big Buddha and Po Lin Monastery** (see pp32–3), or take a ride in the **Ngong Ping 360 Cable Car** (see p49).

Have a vegetarian lunch at the monastery, or take a picnic. The area around Ngong Ping is great for gentle rambles with a view, as well as some serious hill climbing up Lantau Peak.

AFTERNOON

If time still permits, take the bus back towards Mui Wo, but jump out at the fantastic, clean and usually deserted beach at **Cheung Sha** (ask the driver to let you know when). Spend a relaxed afternoon paddling, swimming and sun-bathing on this glorious stretch of golden sand.

From here it's a short ride back into Mui Wo. Slake your afternoon hunger at **Café Isara** (see p121), which offers a selection of Thai and western food.

Before catching the return ferry, squeeze in a drink at the **China Bear** (see p121), a convivial bar near the ferry pier.

See map on pp116–17 ←

Scenic Spots

1 Tai O Village, Lantau
The old fishing village (see p117) on the remote north-west coast is the last settlement in the territory with a significant number of stilt houses, some almost as small as play houses.

2 Any Ferry Aft Deck
Gain some perspective on the dramatic skyline of the islands. Star Ferries (see pp18–19) offer the best chance to capture the dramatic sky-scrapers of central Hong Kong.

3 Po Toi Rock Formations
Head to the remote island of Po Toi (see p119) for breathtaking yellow-rounded cliffs that surround it. Once home to the fishing com-munity, the islands offer some great places to explore, trails to hike and amazing coastal scenery.

4 Cheung Chau Harbour
Handsome, high-prowed fishing boats, squat sampans and busy boatyards are just some of the sights found here (see pp30–31).

5 Big Buddha on Lantau
If the landscape wasn't enough, the mighty Buddha (see pp32–3) cements this island's photo-genic status.

Big Buddha statue on Lantau Island

6 Ngong Ping 360 Cable Car
MAP B5 ▪ Lantau Island ▪ 3666 0606 ▪ Adm ▪ www.np360.com.hk
The 25-minute cable-car ride (see p49) provides one of the best photo opportunities in Hong Kong. From the car, you can see out over Lantau North Country Park, the South China Sea, the Tung Chung Valley and the rest of the surrounding area.

7 Street Art in Peng Chau
MAP C5 ▪ Wing On St, Peng Chau
A converted leather factory, now home to colourful street art, is somewhat of a surprise tucked into the peaceful lanes of Peng Chau. Bonus points for every hidden pop culture reference you spot.

8 View of Airport and Macau Bridge
MAP B5
Take a powerful lens on a clear day to get decent shots of the airport from Lantau Peak. The summit also offers terrific views down onto the monastery and surrounding country.

9 Sunset on Lamma Island's beaches
MAP D5–E6
The mostly residential Lamma Island is a great place to visit for a leisurely hike. Finish off the day with a pit stop at one of the island's beaches just before dusk for some breathtaking sunset views.

10 Tsing Ma Bridge Lookout Point
MAP D4
If big construction projects are your subjects of choice, then head to the free Airport Core Programme Exhibition Centre in Ting Kau. The viewing platform on the roof offers a great opportunity to photograph the Tsing Ma (see p39) and Ting Kau bridges.

Places to Eat and Drink

PRICE CATEGORIES

For a three-course meal for one with half a bottle of wine (or equivalent meal) and extra charges.

$ under $250 $$ $250–600 $$$ over $600

1 Tin Yin Dessert, Cheung Chau

MAP C6 ▪ 9 Tai Hing Tai Rd ▪ 9525 7165 ▪ No credit cards ▪ Closed Mon ▪ $

Waterside canteen serving refreshing and unusual treats – try the sago with jelly and coconut milk.

Casual façade of China Bear, Lantau

2 China Bear, Lantau

MAP C5 ▪ G/F Mui Wo Centre ▪ 2984 9720 ▪ $

Missed the ferry? Never mind. Nip around the corner for the cheap lunch specials and 30 kinds of bottled and draught beer.

3 McSorley's Ale House, Lantau

MAP C4 ▪ Shop G11A, G/F D'Deck, Discovery Bay ▪ 2987 8280 ▪ $$

Popular with home-sick expats craving the taste of familiar dishes, such as fish and chips, pies, curries and hearty Sunday roasts. There's also Guinness and a choice of real ales to wash it all down.

4 Cheung Chau Windsurfing Centre Outdoor Café

MAP C6 ▪ 1 Hai Pak Rd, Cheung Chau ▪ 2981 8316 ▪ Closed Wed ▪ $

At this café, the menu includes "all-day" breakfast, snacks and mainly Western starters that are are as good as the view.

5 Café Isara, Lantau

MAP B6 ▪ Shop 3, G/F, 18A Mui Wo Ferry Pier Rd, Mui Wo ▪ 2470 1966 ▪ $

Feast on Thai food at this elegant harbour-side restaurant, loved by Mui Wo residents and visitors alike.

6 Rainbow Seafood, Lamma

MAP E6 ▪ 16–20 First St, Sok Kwu Wan ▪ 2982 8100 ▪ $$

One of Lamma's better places for a full seafood splurge with a harbour view. Very popular with the locals.

7 Bookworm Café, Lamma

MAP D5 ▪ 79 Yung Shue Wan Main St ▪ 2982 4838 ▪ $

This place wears its organic, veggie and vegan heart on its sleeve, with its twee slogans to peace, love and tofu on its walls. The service is friendly and the fresh food and fruit juices are exceptional.

8 Lamma Seaview Man Fung Seafood, Lamma

MAP D5 ▪ 5 Main St, Yung Shue Wan ▪ 2982 0719 ▪ $$$

Neither the best nor the cheapest seafood on Lamma, but the setting – overlooking the bay – is superb.

9 Cheung Kee, Cheung Chau

MAP C6 ▪ 83 Praya St ▪ 2981 8078 ▪ No credit cards ▪ $

Somewhat shabby premises, but the noodles, dumplings and wontons are just right. There's no signage in English, but it's easy to find, just by the ferry pier – look for the sign "1959".

10 Ming Kee Seafood, Po Toi

MAP F6 ▪ Tai Wan ▪ 2849 7038 ▪ No credit cards ▪ $$

Run by a restaurateur and his daughters, this is Po Toi's best restaurant *(see p119)*. Reach it by junk or from Stanley and Aberdeen.

See map on pp116–17

🔟 Macau

A-Ma Temple, near Avenida da República

Gambling is indisputably the main attraction in Macau, and the area claims to earn more revenue from its 30-odd casinos than Las Vegas does, catering mainly to weekend visitors from Hong Kong and, increasingly, mainland China. However, the Portuguese also had 400 years of rich history here, leaving behind whole districts of cobbled lanes and Iberian architecture. The Indigenous cuisine, which fuses together Chinese and Portuguese elements, is another major draw.

MACAU

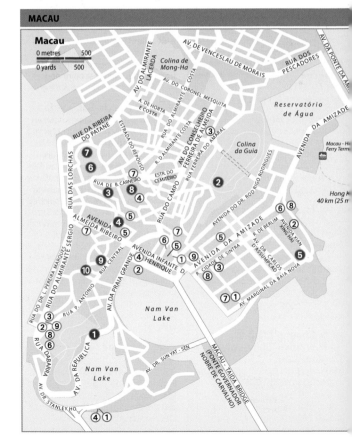

1 Avenida da República

The graceful boughs of banyan trees stretch all across this elegant avenue, shading its candy-coloured pageant of colonial-era architecure. Unlike in Hong Kong, many of Macau's historic piles survive in excellent condition. At the striking fort-turned-hotel of Pousada de São Tiago, the road becomes Rua de S. Tiago da Barra; follow it to the A-Ma Temple and the Maritime Museum *(see p126)*.

Guia Lighthouse, Macau's highest point

2 Guia Lighthouse

The most visible of Macau's landmarks has kept its lonely vigil on Guia Hill since 1638, its flashing beacon beckoning to everyone from Portuguese traders to ferocious pirates and marauding Dutch navy boats. Catch the cable car up the hill, take in the 360-degree panorama from Macau's highest point and enjoy a leisurely stroll back down.

3 Ruinas de São Paulo
Museum of Sacred Art: open 9am–6pm daily (last adm 5:30pm); closed Tue pm

The façade and mosaic floor are all that remain of Macau's grandest church, perched atop a flight of stone steps and propped up by a viewing platform. In its heyday, it was hailed as the greatest monument to Christianity in the East. It caught fire during a typhoon in 1835, and only due to structural work in the early 1990s did the façade survive. Portuguese influence is evident in the artifacts in the Museum of Sacred Art's collection.

Ruinas de São Paulo

The colourful Largo do Senado

4 Largo do Senado
Leal Senado: 163 Avenida Almeida Ribeiro

Brightly painted Colonial buildings and slightly psychedelic paving make this square in the heart of Macau a favourite with photographers. At one end sits the Leal Senado, or Loyal Senate, now the seat of the municipal government but once the Portuguese headquarters. It was thus named because Macau refused to recognize the 17th-century Spanish occupation of Portugal.

5 Cultural Centre
Avenida Xian Xing Hai ■ 2870 0699 ■ Open 11am–7pm daily ■ www.ccm.gov.mo

This elegant building was designed and constructed in time for the December 1999 Handover to China. In fact, the actual ceremony took place behind the centre in a temporary structure designed to look like a giant Chinese lantern. The centre is the focal point for the Macau Arts Festival in March. The only mystery is why there is what appears to be a ski jump on the roof.

6 Protestant Cemetery
Open 8:30am–5:30pm daily

More interesting than it sounds – you might find yourself spending hours wandering this grave-dotted grove, reading inscriptions to travellers, plague-doomed sailors and colonial adventurers. Those lain to rest here include painter George Chinnery (the Mandarin Oriental's bar in Hong Kong is named after him) and Robert Morrison, the first Protestant to venture to China in search of converts.

7 Camões Garden and Grotto
Praça de Luís de Camões ■ Open 6am–10pm daily

The author of the 16th-century Portuguese epic *The Lusiads* may never have visited Macau, but don't try telling the local Portuguese. Luís Vaz de Camões specialized in over-blown, patriotic verse – a bust of him peers through the grotto's gloom. Old men take their caged birds to the gardens in the morning.

8 Fortaleza do Monte
Open 7am–7pm daily

These walls bounded the original Portuguese settlement in Macau – a well-stocked fort – which its inhabitants boasted could withstand years of siege. The sternest test came in the year 1622 when the Dutch, who had coveted Macau for years, made their move, only to be decisively beaten. The Portuguese military was based here up until 1966, at which point Portugal decided it was more politic to be administrators of Macau rather than gun-toting colonialists.

MACAU'S HISTORY

Macau was settled by the Portuguese in 1557 as a trading base and centre for Christianity. Colonial coats of arms can still be seen in Fortaleza do Monte. Macau was nearly taken by the Dutch in 1622, and struggled to survive for the next 250 years. The Portuguese tried to re-establish power in the mid-19th century, annexing neighbouring islands Taipa and Coloane. It could never compete with Hong Kong, however, and gambling, sex work and opium remained the primary pursuits here. Mao rejected a Portuguese attempt to return the enclave in the 1970s, but it was eventually handed back to China in 1999.

Façade of Dom Pedro V Theatre

⑨ Dom Pedro V Theatre
Largo de Santo Agostinho
- Macau Tourism Office: 2833 3000
- Open 10am–6pm Wed–Mon

The first Western-style lyric theatre in the East, the Dom Pedro opened in 1858 designed in Neo-Classical style. It is still used to host performances. The hike up the hill is worth it for a look at a piece of theatrical history.

⑩ St Joseph's Seminary and Church
Rua do Seminario ■ Church: open 10am–5pm daily; Seminary: closed to the public

The Jesuits constructed this chapel between 1746 and 1758, modelled on the Church of the Gesù in Rome. Its dedication plaque lists Portuguese King João V, Macau Bishop Hilario de St Rosa and Chinese Qing-dynasty Emperor Qian Long. The original bells still ring out, and fascinating Catholic artifacts can be found within.

Ornate altar, St Joseph's Seminary

A DAY IN MACAU

▶ **MORNING**

Catch a taxi to the **Ruinas de São Paulo** (see p123) in the heart of Macau, pose for a picture on the steps in front, then lose yourself in the surrounding streets full of Chinese and antiques shops. The red lacquered trunks and cabinets, old teak tables and chairs are all cheaper here than in Hong Kong's antiques shops.

When your feet start to protest, take a cab across the causeways to Coloane island and a lunch at **Fernando's** (see p129). Get a large jug of piquant sangria in, then go for the tasty fried chicken, garlic prawns, clams and sardines. The bread is hot and moreish, and the Portuguese salad is pure bliss.

AFTERNOON

Walk off lunch on **Hac Sa Beach** (see p126) or make your way to the minibus outside Fernando's and travel to **Taipa Village** (see p126), which is home to picturesque houses and shops.

Then grab another taxi and head to the **Macau Tower** (see p126) for magnificent views of Macau and across the sea to Taipa, Coloane and the Cotai Strip. If you're feeling adventurous, you could try the Skywalk around the outer rim or even the bungee jump from the Observation Deck.

If you have the stamina, make your way to Avenida Dr Sun Yat Sen and its many bars for a night on the tiles or straightaway head to the swish bars of the **Cotai Strip** (see p127).

See map on pp122–3 ←

The Best of the Rest

Macau Tower, above Nam Van Lake

1 Macau Tower
Nam Van Lakes area ▪ 2893 3339
Dominating Macau's skyline, this tower was built by casino mogul Dr Stanley Ho. At 338 m (1,107 ft), it just beats the Eiffel Tower and forms the centre of a convention and restaurant complex. The Skywalker X and the glass-floored revolving restaurant are not for the faint of heart.

2 Pousada de Coloane
Cheoc Van Praia, Coloane ▪ 2888 2143
Macau's first beachfront hotel is a top spot for a few cold drinks when the sun is shining.

3 Lou Lim Ieoc Garden
10 Estrada de Adolfo Loureiro ▪ Open 6am–midnight daily
Shady trees, benches and lotus ponds; a good place to unwind.

4 Macau Museum
Fortaleza do Monte ▪ 2835 7911 ▪ Open 10am–6pm Tue–Sun ▪ Adm (free on Tue & 15th of each month)
Good displays on the history and architecture of the region.

5 São Domingos
Largo do Domingos ▪ 2836 7706 ▪ Open 10am–6pm daily
The pale yellow late 16th-century Spanish-style church towers over the Largo do Senado square. White ants forced major renovations in the mid-1990s. More than 300 sacred works of art are in the bell tower's museum.

6 A-Ma Temple
Rua do Almirante Sergio ▪ Open 7am–6pm daily
Images of junks decorate this pretty collection of halls dedicated to the patron deity of sailors, after whom the name "Macau" is derived.

7 Rua da Felicidade
The "street of happiness" once teemed with brothels, hence its bestowed name. It's now a thoroughfare full of cheap restaurants.

8 Maritime Museum
Largo do Pagode da Barra ▪ 2859 5481 ▪ Open 10am–6pm Wed–Mon (last adm 5:30pm) ▪ Adm
This is the place to head if you are interested in learning about Macau's colourful seagoing past.

9 Old Taipa Village
A destination that packs in something for everyone, this charming village features rustic houses that help retain its historical feel. The cobbled colonial streets that flank Rua Correia da Silva are perfect to stroll along on a lazy day.

10 Hac Sa Beach
Coloane
Enjoy a stroll around the headland on this black-mineral-sand beach.

Casinos

① **Sands Cotai Central**
Estrada do Istmo ▪ 2886 6888
▪ www.sandscotaicentral.com
This resort combines 4 hotels,
20 dining options, shopping
and gambling on a vast scale.

② **Sands**
Largo de Monte Carlo 203
▪ 2888 3388 ▪ www.sandsmacao.com
The first of the Vegas-style mega-
casinos to arrive on the waterfront.

③ **StarWorld Macau**
Avenida da Amizade ▪ 2838
3838 ▪ www.starworldmacau.com
This luxurious hotel has a distinctive
Asian style and a large casino with
an impressive LED wall. There are
live shows every night.

④ **City of Dreams**
Estrada de Istmo, Cotai Strip
▪ 8868 6688 ▪ www.cityofdreams
macau.com
This opulent mega-casino is aimed
at those with a penchant for ostenta-
tious interiors and deluxe facilities.

⑤ **Grand Lisboa**
Avenida de Lisboa ▪ 2828 3838
▪ www.grandlisboahotels.com
Casino mogul Dr Stanley Ho
built this extravagant party palace,
complete with a giant casino and
15 restaurants, next door. Nowhere
says "Macau bling" quite like this
huge golden tower.

⑥ **The Venetian**
Estrada da Baía de N Senhora
da Esperança, Taipa ▪ 2882 8888
▪ www.venetianmacao.com
The full Las Vegas experience has
been transported to the tropics. Live
shows and big-brand shopping along
air-conditioned streets provide a
welcome break from gambling.

Indoor shopping at The Venetian

⑦ **MGM Grand**
Avenida Dr Sun Yat Sen, NAPE
▪ 8802 8888 ▪ Open 24 hours daily
An astonishing rippling façade, a
fancy spa and a vast gambling hall in
the style of a Portuguese town square
can be found at MGM Grand.

⑧ **Wynn**
Rua Cidade de Sintra, NAPE
▪ 2888 9966 ▪ www.wynnmacau.com
This is one of the most lavish casinos
in Macau. The interior is decked out
with floral carpets and chandeliers.

⑨ **Kampek Paradise Casino**
51 Rua de Foshan ▪ www.
paradise-macau.com
The loyal clientele of local punters
here can be rude to tourists and
flashy Hong Kongers.

⑩ **Macau Jockey Club**
Estrada Gov Albano da Oliveira,
Taipa ▪ 2882 0868 ▪ Race meetings
Fri evening & Sat–Sun ▪ www.mjc.
mo ▪ Adm
A bit less glamorous than its
high-tech, cashed-up Hong Kong
counterpart, but just as much fun.

Extravagant Grand Lisboa hotel

See map on pp122–3 ←

Cafés, Bars and Clubs

Vida Rica Bar at the Mandarin Oriental Macau

1 Vida Rica Bar
Mandarin Oriental Macau, Avenida Dr Sun Yat Sen
Great for watching Macau's movers and shakers, this extravagantly styled bar has an arty interior and fabulous harbour views.

2 SKY 21
21/F, AIA Tower, 251A–301 Avenida Comercial de Macau ▪ 2822 2122
Located close to the centre, SKY 21 has a dining area, a live music venue, plus a roof terrace with great views across the city and the sea. Splurge, party, mingle, or simply spend some time under the stars.

3 Para Club
Level 2, City of Dreams ▪ 6333 6330
This two-floor club is complete with a laser-lit dance pool, resident DJs, and five VIP rooms.

4 360 Café
60/F Macau Tower, Lago San Vai ▪ 8988 8622
This revolving bar, restaurant and café at the top of the Macau Tower offers peerless views over the old city, the sea and islands.

5 Oskar's Bar
G/F Holiday Inn Hotel, Rua de Pequim ▪ 2878 3333
A mix of tourists and locals gather at this typical hotel-style bar, as well as the odd exponent of the world's oldest profession. Major sports events are shown on flat-screen TVs.

6 Vasco
2/F Grand Lapa Hotel, Avenida da Amizade ▪ 8793 3831
Enjoy tasty tapas-style fare and imaginative cocktails at Vasco. Best for a quiet evening drink.

7 CheChe Café
B/F, 70A Rua Tomás Vieira ▪ 6288 0857
A low-key joint frequented by both locals and expats who come to socialize and have fun.

8 D2
Macau Fisherman's Wharf, Edf. New Orleans III ▪ 2872 3777
One of the city's liveliest dance clubs, D2 features a mix of music, with bar-top pole dancers at weekends.

9 Flame Bar
Level 2, Hard Rock Hotel, City of Dreams, Cotai ▪ 8868 6688
A fine selection of cocktails and an irrepressibly upscale party vibe feature at this lounge and club.

10 The Blissful Carrot
1/F, 568 Olympic Avenue, Va Nam Industrial Building ▪ 6298 8433
This homey café serves vegetarian and vegan food made with the freshest organic ingredients.

Places to Eat

PRICE CATEGORIES

For a three-course meal for one with half a bottle of wine (or equivalent meal) and extra charges.

$ under $250 $$ $250–600 $$$ over $600

1 The 8 Restaurant
2/F Grand Lisboa, Avenida de Lisboa ▪ 8803 7788 ▪ $$$

Enjoy superb Chinese food at this modern, lavish restaurant with three Michelin stars. One of 15 dining options at the Grand Lisboa.

2 A Lorcha
Rua do Almirante Sergio 289 ▪ 2831 3193 ▪ $$

Fine Macanese cooking, which blends the cuisines of East and West, is on offer here. Specialities include the spicy grilled African chicken, *bacalhau* (baked codfish) and *caldo verde* (potato purée soup). Book ahead.

3 Litoral
Rua do Almirante Sergio 261 ▪ 2896 7878 ▪ $$

One of the best places for organic and Mediterranean fare. Try the tasty African Chicken or stuffed prawns.

4 Solmar
Avenida da Praia Grande 512 ▪ 2888 1881 ▪ $$

An old favourite among locals. Try the rich seafood soup with chunks of codfish that melt in your mouth.

5 Ou Mun
12 Travesa de Sao Domingos ▪ 2837 2207 ▪ $$

A top spot for heart-starting morning coffee and Portuguese food.

6 Robuchon au Dôme
43/F Grand Lisboa, Avenida de Lisboa ▪ 8803 7878 ▪ $$$

This exquisite fine-dining parlour has not only three Michelin stars but also superlative city views.

7 Clube Militar de Macau
Avenida da Praia Grande 975 ▪ 2871 4004 ▪ $$

Built to cater for army bigwigs, the Military Club is one of the best examples of classical European architecture in Asia. Gourmet Portuguese cuisine is on offer here, and the lunch buffet is great value.

8 Espaco Lisboa
Rua dos Gaivotas 8, Coloane ▪ 2888 2226 ▪ $$

Tucked away in a Coloane village and presided over by the Portuguese chef-owner, this rustic restaurant is a reminder of pre-development, sleepy Macau.

9 Casa do Porco Preto
G/F, 5C Fong Son San Chun Building, 310 Rua de Almirante Sergio ▪ 2896 6313 ▪ $$

A Portuguese restaurant offering an unbeatable farm-to-table experience at accessible prices. Dig into the likes of grilled meat and suckling pig.

10 Fernando's
Praia Hac Sa 9, Coloane ▪ 2888 2264 (booking recommended) ▪ No credit cards ▪ $$

This is the perfect place for a long, lazy lunch. Succulent roast chicken, grilled sardines, killer sangria and garlic prawns to die for. Shady, outdoor seating for cooler days.

Outdoor seating at Fernando's

See map on pp122–3 ←

🔟 Shenzhen

Within living memory, Shenzhen, located just across the border of the New Territories, was a minor township in Communist China, its communal fisheries set in extraordinary juxtaposition to capitalist Hong Kong. Yet Shenzhen (or "Shumchun") has undergone a major shift from quiet backwater to booming metropolis since 1979. The reason for this dramatic transformation is the city's status as a free-trading Special Economic Zone, which has created wealth and attracted entrepreneurs and workers from all over China. Today, it mostly functions as a business center and transportation hub – but, despite the city's development, several places of historical interest and areas of natural beauty remain.

Interior of the five-storey Luo Hu Commercial City

SHENZHEN

0 km — 2
0 miles — 2
20 km (12.5 miles) 7

TANG'AO

Xili Reservoir

TIANLIAOZAI

Meilin Reservoir

GUANGDONG PROVINCE

XIAMEILIN

LONGJING

Liánhuá Shan Par

WUWU

NANTOU

6
5 4 8

GUIMIAOXINCUN

10

FUTIAN

NANSHAN

HAUKOI

Deep Bay (Shenzhen Bay)

9
8 10
SHEKOU
4

Mai Po Nature Reserve

1 Luo Hu Commercial City
By border stn

Right by the border station, this large mall is the most convenient place to shop in Shenzhen. Inside its teeming five storeys are virtually all the consumer goods you could ever desire, in exhaustive and exhausting quantities. The brands are either Chinese (often of solid build) or fake Western (take your chances). Countless stalls sell all manner of clothes, footwear, jewellery, watches, accessories and electronic goods. A huge textiles market is on the fifth floor. Expect to haggle over prices: offer no more than 10 per cent of the first asking price to start with.

2 Dong Men District
A couple of miles N of Luo Hu

If you have the energy to tackle it, a vast expanse of clothes shops awaits you in the sprawling Dong Men district. From graphic tees to jeans to accessories, this is a shopping paradise. At the eastern edge of Dong Men is a footbridge leading to another huge fabric market, which is located above a food market. There's no English signposting here, though, so be sure to have the destination written down in Chinese.

Fairy Lake Botanical Garden

3 Fairy Lake Botanical Garden
Liantang District ■ 2573 8430 ■ Open 4am–9:30pm; museum: open 9am–5pm ■ Adm (free before 8am and after 6pm)

9 km (6 miles) east of the border crossing, lies the 500-hectare (1235-acre) garden around Fairy Lake (Xianhu in Chinese). Featuring 8,000 tropical species and 12 themed sub-gardens, it's a lovely place to admire Southeast Asia's range of flora. Visit the Paleontological Museum and hire a boat on the lake or explore the Hongfa Buddhist Temple in the hills.

4 China Folk Culture Village
Overseas Chinese Town ■ 2660 0626 ■ Open 9am–9:30pm daily ■ Adm (includes Splendid China)

With re-creations of traditional Chinese villages, which pay tribute to the country's different ethnic minority groups, this spot is a modern-day cultural microcosm of a lesser-seen side of China.

Folk culture performer

YICUN

QINGSHUIHE

Bijia Shan Park

LUO HU

5 km (3 miles)

2

2

5

7 9 3
1
6

3

NEW TERRITORIES

KWU TUNG

SHEUNG SHUI

SHEK WU WAI

5 Window of the World
Overseas Chinese Town
■ 2660 8000 ■ Open 10am–7pm
daily ■ Adm ■ en.szwwco.com

Complimenting Shenzhen's appetite
for theme parks, the surreal Window
of the World is a reduction (literally
and metaphorically) of the real world.
Mount Fuji becomes a 6-m (20-ft) slag
heap, tourists pose in Thai national
dress in front of the Taj Mahal and,
poignantly, Manhattan retains its
World Trade Center. Live shows are
put on at set times on most "conti-
nents". There's also a Grand Canyon
flume ride and an indoor ski slope
with artificial snow.

6 Happy Valley
Overseas Chinese Town
■ 2694 9184 ■ Open 9:30am–9:30pm
daily ■ Adm

This theme park gives Hong Kong's
Ocean Park a run for its money, with
the bonus of a tidal pool, adrenalin-
inducing rides such as the Space
Shot, an assault course and martial
arts demonstrations. Weekends are
best avoided as the queues are long.

7 Mission Hills Golf Club
Mission Hills Rd, Guanlan
town ■ Reservations: 2802 0888
■ Regular shuttle buses from HK,
Kowloon, Shenzhen and Dongguan
■ www.missionhillschina.com

Several Hong Kong executives
come across the border to play at
this 5-star, 216-hole golf club, the
largest in the world. The luxurious
resort also has 18 tennis courts
among other facilities.

Miniature model at Splendid China

8 Splendid China
Overseas Chinese Town ■ 2660
0626 ■ Open 10am–6pm daily ■ Adm
(includes China Folk Cultural Village)

On show here are the architectural
wonders of China, including stunning
re-creations of Beijing's Imperial
Palace, the Terracotta Warriors of
Xi'an and the Great Wall.

9 Bargain Beauty Treatments

When you reach breaking point with
all the shopping malls and theme
parks, rest and refresh yourself with
an exceptionally cheap foot or back
massage. A vast range of treatments
is available at Luo Hu Commercial
City (see p131). Hotel health centres
offer the assurance of professional
reflexology and traditional massage.

10 Shenzhen Bay Park
Binhai Dadao and Wanghai Lu

More than 10 km (6.2 miles) of the
Shenzhen Bay shoreline has been
turned into a park with cycling paths
and free Wi-Fi in some areas. On a
clear day you can see all the way
to Hong Kong.

Golfers at Mission Hills Golf Club

Places to Eat and Drink

PRICE CATEGORIES
For a three-course meal for one with half
a bottle of wine and extra charges. Prices
are quoted in Chinese yuan.
....
¥ under ¥180   ¥¥ ¥180–400   ¥¥¥ over ¥400

1 Xingli
116 Fuhua San Rd, Futian
■ 2222 2222 ■ ¥¥¥

The Chinese restaurant at the swanky
Ritz-Carlton Hotel offers delicate
Chiu Chow cuisine, originating from
the Chaoshan region of China, as
well as a selection of Cantonese
and Schezuan dishes.

2 Jingyi Chaguan
7/F Jingtang Dasha, 3038
Bao'an Nan Lu, Luo Hu ■ 2558
6555 ■ ¥

Elegant vegetarian teahouse
restaurant that attracts Buddhist
monks as well as resident
foreigners. Try the dim sum.

**3 Golden Peninsula
Chiu Chow**
Block B, 1/F Lido Hotel, 2007 Dong
Men Nan Lu, Luo Hu ■ 8225 9988
■ ¥¥

A central location that's easy to find,
a clear English menu and polite staff
all make this one of the best Chinese
restaurants in town.

4 Muslim Noodle House
8 Taizi Rd, Shekou ■ 8222 9318
■ No credit cards ■ ¥

Enjoy large, steaming bowls of soup
made with tasty, hand-pulled noodles.
There is also a variety of other traditional Uighur dishes on offer here that
are easy on the wallet.

5 Nanyuan Lu
Nanyuan Lu, Futian ■ ¥

Like most major cities in China,
Shenzhen has an active Muslim
community. This row of restaurants
serves delicious mutton kebabs,
pilau rice and naan to hungry
tourists and locals alike.

Revolving restaurant, 360°

6 360°
31F Shangri-La Hotel, 1002
Jianshe Lu ■ 8396 1380 ■ ¥¥¥

With great views of Shenzhen,
especially at night, the revolving
restaurant atop the Shangri-La
Hotel *(see p148)* has excellent steaks
and a good collection of fine wines.

7 Laurel Restaurant
Shop 5010, 5/F Luo Hu
Commercial City ■ 8232 3668 ■ ¥¥

This terrific classic Cantonese
restaurant tends to be packed
all day, but it's worth the wait.

8 The Terrace
Seaworld Square, Shekou
■ 2682 9105 ■ ¥¥

Lively restaurant with a bar and
nightclub that serves Thai food in the
Shekou district, which is the harbourside bolthole of Shenzhen's expats.

9 Gold Coast
Hai Bin Commercial Bldg,
Seaworld Square, Shekou ■ 2667
6968 ■ ¥¥

One of the best places in town
to enjoy a steak along with good
Aussie wine.

10 McCawley's
Shop No.118 Seaworld Square,
Shekou ■ 2668 4496 ■ ¥¥

Irish pub chain that serves good
pub grub and imported beers,
including Guinness.

See map on pp130–31

𝗧𝗢𝗣 𝟭𝟬 Guangzhou

China's two great revolutions, republican and communist, were born in Guangzhou, which indicates the temperament of this sprawling southern Chinese capital. Far distant from Beijing, the city has gone its own wilful way, and there is still the insouciance of a people who answer to no one. The modern city is at the mercy of miasmic smog and yammering traffic, but it also has enormous personality, from the soaring Canton Tower, with the world's highest Ferris wheel, to the Han dynasty tombs, plentiful temples, and the charm of Shamian Island's faded 19th-century terraces.

① Wandering Among the Gei

Perhaps the simplest yet most worthwhile thing to do in Guangzhou is to wander aimlessly along its *gei*, the narrow labyrinthine alleyways between the ancient ramshackle houses in the older parts of town. The streets from Shamian Island up as far as Liwan District are especially interesting. Strolling down these byways gives a sense of the everyday life that has carried on here for hundreds of years. Absorb yourself in the minutiae of domestic life and small-scale industries, such as beauty treatments, maybe in the form of eyebrow pluck-ing with a simple piece of cotton.

A Guangzhou *gei*

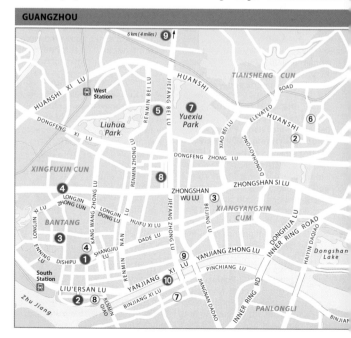

GUANGZHOU

Walkers admire a sculpture on a leafy Shamian Island path

2 Shamian Island
Metro Huangsha

The small islet located in southwest Guangzhou long served as the main gateway to China, the only place where merchants and diplomats were allowed to do business with the Empire. Today it's a leafy haven, well restored and beautified, with good accommodation and dining options, as well as quiet riverside walks.

3 Hua Lin Temple and Jade Market
North of Xiajiu Lu, East of Wen Nan Wen Lu, metro Changshou Lu ■ Temple: open 8am–5pm daily

An extensive jade market surrounds the Buddhist temple of Hua Lin, which is also worth a quick visit. The jade on sale here is cheaper than in Hong Kong, although you'll need to be an expert to separate the rare real jade from the fake. There are several antiques stores and jade and amber sellers west of Kangwang Zhong Lu and north of Changshang Xi Lu.

Buddha statue, Hua Lin Temple

4 Chen Clan Academy
34 Enlong Li, Zhongshan Qi Lu, metro Chen Clan Academy ■ 8181 4559 ■ Open 8:30am–5:30pm daily ■ Adm

With Chen being the most common family name in the area, it's no surprise that the many groupings of local Chens built a sprawling temple in the 1890s. It's worth a look if you haven't visited the ancestral halls in the New Territories. An impressive feature is the ornate friezes on the roof, depicting Confucian moral tales. There are also displays of jade, bone and other crafts, some for sale. The leafy courtyards give peace and shade.

XIANLI NAN LU

HUANSHI

TIANHE LU →

ONGFENG ZHONG LU

ZHONGSHAN SAN LU

GUANGZHOU LU

6 km (3.5 miles)

5

HUANGPU LU

10

ZHUJIANG

SIYOU NEW ROAD

WUYANGCUN

HUACHENG LU

LINJIANG LU

Ershatou Island

6

5 km (3 miles)

1

Zhu Jiang

0 kilometres 1

0 miles 1

DONG LU

⑤ Nanyue Tomb
867 Jiefang Bei Lu ■ **3618 2920**
■ Open 9am–5:30pm daily (last adm
4:45pm) ■ Adm

A well-presented museum preserves
the burial tomb and artifacts of one
of the kings of the Southern Yue, who
ruled the area in the 2nd century BC.
Well signposted in Chinese and in
English, the tomb offers a glimpse of
a culturally sophisticated society. Fine
ceramic pillows and exquisite pack-
aging materials from later dynasties
feature among the displays.

⑥ Guangdong Museum of Art
Luhu Lu 13, Ersha Island ■ **8735
1468** ■ Open 9am–5pm Tue–Sun
■ **www.gdmoa.org** ■ Adm

This is probably still the largest art
museum in China. The exhibitions
cover both ancient and contemporary
Chinese art.

⑦ Yuexiu Park
**Park: Metro Yuexiu Park; open
6am–9pm daily** ■ **Museum: open
9am–5pm daily; adm**

This lovely park contains a sculpture
of the *Five Rams*, the symbol of
Guangzhou, and a monument to Sun
Yat-sen, the revered "father of modern China". The Municipal
Museum, tracing the
history of Guangzhou,
is housed in the
Zhen Hai Tower,
the last remnant
of the city's 14th-
century walls.

Five Rams,
Yuexiu Park

Temple of the Six Banyan Trees

⑧ Bright Filial Piety Temple and Six Banyan Trees
Both on Liurong Lu ■ **Bright Filial
Piety: open 6:30am–5pm; Six Banyan
Trees: open 9am–5pm daily** ■ Adm

Bright Filial Piety Temple (Guangxiao
Si) was a royal temple as far back as
the 2nd century BC, and is thought
to have served as a Buddhist shrine
since the 4th century AD. However, the
buildings that stand here today were
built in the 17th century. Sit beneath
ancient fig trees in quiet courtyards.
The Temple of the Six Banyan Trees
(Liurong Si), located close by, has
the oldest and largest pagoda in
Guangzhou, standing 55 m (180 ft) tall
but, sadly, the banyan trees have died.

⑨ White Cloud Mountain
Overlooking the city haze is a
sprawling wooded area dominated by
a series of ridges and peaks, which
offers open space and fresh air.

⑩ River Trips
Escape the fumes and look
back on the city from the river. A
number of operators offer cruises.
Try an evening trip on the *White
Swan*, a lovely old masted yacht.

Places to Eat and Drink

PRICE CATEGORIES
For a three-course meal for one with half
a bottle of wine, taxes and extra charges.
Prices are quoted in Chinese yuan.
....
¥ under ¥180 ¥¥ ¥180–400 ¥¥¥ over ¥400

1 Ming Court
Langham Place Hotel, 638
Xingang Dong Rd, Haizhu ▪ 8916
3588 ▪ ¥¥¥
The menu at Ming Court features
high-class traditional Chinese dishes,
which are served in modern yet
culturally apt surroundings.

2 The Paddy Field
Central Plaza, 38 Huale Lu
▪ 8360 1379 ▪ ¥¥
One of the most popular expatriate
hangouts, this cheekily named
restaurant offers traditional Irish
fare. After a diet of noodles, rack
of lamb with mint sauce can come
as a shock.

3 Haidilao Hotpot
5/F Grandbuy Bldg, 395
Zhongshan 4 Lu ▪ 8302 7255 ▪ ¥
On the corner of the pedestrianized
Beijing Lu, this restaurant gives
an excellent introduction to fiery
Szrchuan cuisine. Hotpot can be
ordered with a yin/yang style divider
for those unsure about spicy food.

4 Guangzhou
2 Wen Chang Nan Lu
▪ 8138 0388 ▪ ¥
The oldest and most famous
restaurant in the city, Guangzhou
is almost always busy. Guests can
choose from a massive menu of
Cantonese dishes.

5 I by Inagiku
5/F W Guangzhou Hotel, 26
Xiancun Lu, Tianhe ▪ 6680 7830 ▪ ¥¥
This large Japanese restaurant is
cleverly laid out, with different areas
serving different styles of food. The
place offers great views of the city
and an all-you-can-eat option.

Tang cu li ji (sweet-and-sour pork)

6 Baiyun Xuan
Bayun Hotel, 367 Huanshi
Donglu ▪ 8333 3998 ▪ ¥¥
A great opportunity to try – among
other Cantonese and Chaozhou
specialities – sweet-and-sour pork
(tang cu li ji) as it should be.

7 Fo Shijie Sushishe
2–8 Niu Nai Chang Jie ▪ 8424
3590 ▪ ¥
Located south of the river, Fo Shijie
Sushishe is considered one of the
best places to try Cantonese vegetarian cuisine.

8 Orient Express
1 Shamian Bei Lu, Shamian
Island ▪ 4436 4070 ▪ ¥¥¥
Enjoy good French cuisine in a luxury
train carriage or in the garden at this
Gallic-owned brasserie.

9 1920 Restaurant and Bar
4/F, 1, Jianshe Liu Ma Lu ▪ 8388
1142 ▪ ¥¥
Expats and locals alike enjoy food with
a strong German influence. There's
also an outdoor terrace near the river.

10 G Bar
Grand Hyatt Guangzhou, 12
Zhujiang West Rd ▪ 8396 1234 ▪ ¥¥¥
This impressive lounge is a stellar
spot for pre- or post-dinner drinks
while enjoying fine city views.

See map on pp134–5 ←

Streetsmart

Neon signs illuminating
Portland Street, Kowloon

Getting Around

Arriving by Air

Most international visitors arrive to Hong Kong by air, flying into **Hong Kong International Airport** on Chek Lap Kok, off Lantau Island, about 30 km (19 miles) northwest of downtown. Airport buses and taxis run around the clock, with the MTR's Airport Express train (5:54am–12:48pm; HK$115) being the fastest way to reach Kowloon and Central.

It is also possible to fly directly into the cities of Macau, Shenzhen and Guangzhou. **Macau International Airport** sits on the east side of Taipa, about 5 km (3 miles) from the old city, handling traffic from China and Southeast Asia. Buses and taxis connect with the centre (15 min), and there's an adjacent ferry terminal for rapid transfers to Hong Kong (1 hr). **Shenzhen International Airport** offers better-value flights to the rest of China compared to flying from Hong Kong. Buses connect the airport with China Travel Service branches in Kowloon and Hong Kong Island (2–3 hr). **Guangzhou Baiyun International Airport** is one of China's busiest; it's 30 km (19 miles) from Guangzhou city, best reached via metro line number 3.

Many airlines fly into Hong Kong. Hong Kong's national carrier is **Cathay Pacific**, offering direct flights to the US, Europe, UK, Australia, China and Southeast Asia. Air fares vary according to the airline and the season. The peak season for international flights is between June and September, when prices are highest. Reasonably priced tickets are also hard to find during the holidays: Chinese New Year and the week-long holiday period after October 1, when it is advisable to book well in advance.

Arriving by Train

For many travellers, train journeys are an excellent way to see the countryside. Trains are punctual, fast and relatively safe, and are a reliable transport option. Hong Kong's long-distance train station is West Kowloon Terminus, just between Kowloon MTR and Austin MTR stations. Express bus services connect it to various destinations around Hong Kong Island, Kowloon and the New Territories. **MTR Intercity** high-speed trains arriving from China terminate here, as do East Rail MTR services from the border at Shenzhen.

Guangzhou has many stations, but **Guangzhou East** (reached via the city's metro) is where you can catch direct trains to Hung Hom. Shenzhen's main train station, where traffic arrives from across China, is at Lo Wu (Luo Hu), immediately across the border from Hong Kong. However, train services from China arrive at the Shenzhen North station and cross at the Futian border crossing. To reach Hong Kong from either, simply walk across the border and ride the MTR East Rail line to Hung Hom. Macau has no rail services.

Trains are usually crowded so it is advisable to either buy your ticket well in advance, or ask your hotel or travel agent to arrange your bookings. On short routes, you may be able to secure a ticket just before departure, but it is safest to buy ahead. Tickets on longer routes sell out fast.

Arriving by Bus

Bus travel is essential for reaching places that are not served by train. Tickets are both easier to procure and are cheaper than train tickets, and there is a wider choice of departure times, stops and itineraries. Buses arrive in Hong Kong via the **Hong Kong-Zhuhai–Macau Bridge (HZMB)**. After arriving at Macau or Zuhai port, board the 24-hr shuttle bus that takes around 40 minutes to cross the bridge to the port border, next to Hong Kong's airport on Lantau. Cross-boundary services such as **Trans-Island Limousine** offer buses that cross the border from Shenzhen Airport (2–3 hrs) to various points in Central and Kowloon.

Arriving by Ferry

Turbojet offers fast catamaran services to Macau, and can be found at the Hong Kong–Macau Ferry Terminal at Sheung Wan on Hong Kong Island and the Kowloon Ferry Terminal on Canton Road, Tsim Sha Tsui. Ferry transfers also operate between Hong Kong International Airport and Guangzhou, Macau and Shenzhen International Airport.

Macau's two seaports are the central Macau Ferry Terminal on Avenida da Amizade, and the Macau Taipa Ferry Terminal, next to the airport on Taipa. Regular ferries run to Hong Kong, Guangzhou and Shenzhen.

Shenzhen's main port is at Shekou, about 10 km (6 miles) west of the Lo Wu border crossing with Hong Kong.

Train Travel

Integrated and efficient, Hong Kong has the best public transport system in the country, making the city easy to get around. The most popular and convenient way to tavel around Hong Kong is using the **MTR** (Mass Transit Railway) network, including subway and overground trains. It has ten lines, over 70 stations and a light-rail system, covering Hong Kong Island's north shore and Kowloon, the New Territories, the airport and northern Lantau Island. Services run daily 6am–midnight, and fares range from HK$2 to HK$57, depending on distance; the Airport Express costs HK$70 to HK$115 each way (multiple tickets are discounted). Most signage is in English.

An **Octopus Card** stored-value electronic ticket gives a discount on MTR fares, and allows you to hop on and off most of the system. You can easily add credit at MTR stations, ferry piers and convenience stores. The fare increases with the distance travelled. If you buy a single ticket, tap it on the turnstile sensor to open the gate. At the end of your journey, feed the ticket into the turnstile to exit the system. If you have an Octopus card, touch the card to the turnstile sensor at the start and end of your journey.

Eating or drinking on Hong Kong's spotless MTR system can result in being fined by the police.

Except for Macau, **Shenzhen** and **Guangzhou** also have extensive metro networks. Safety and hygiene measures, timetables, ticket information, transport maps, and more can be obtained from the websites for each city's transport body.

Buses

Hong Kong city bus networks are extensive, easy to use and a cheap option for getting around, though traffic can be bad. **Hong Kong City Buses** run from 6am to midnight daily (with a few all-night services). Route itineraries are displayed at each stop. Octopus cards are valid on all services; otherwise, you pay upon boarding and fares are worked out in relation to distance travelled. If paying by cash, ensure you have the exact change. Maps of bus routes are widely available,

especially in and around train stations.

Macau's buses (which run 7am–11pm daily) are also inexpensive; most routes cost just MOP$3–4 and you will need the exact change. Buses in Shenzhen and Guangzhou are crowded and slow – it's better to take the metro.

Trams

Hong Kong Island's historic double-decker **trams** run along the north shore between Kennedy Town and Shau Kei Wan. They're a fun and inexpensive way to get around, costing about HK$2.60 a ride – pay the exact amount as you get off, or swipe your Octopus card.

In addition to the double-decker trams, the **Peak Tram** in Hong Kong is a funicular railway running from Central to the Peak Tower complex, where impeccable views await.

Taxis

Colour-coded **taxis** are everywhere in Hong Kong: a vast majority of taxis are red, though you'll also spot green taxis in the New Territories and blue ones on Lantau Island. Fares for red taxis start at around HK$24, then increase by HK$1.70 per 656 ft (200 m) from the airport if you're going to Hong Kong Island. Excess luggage and the cross-harbour tunnels incur surcharges.

Guests staying at hotels can also ask the reception desk to summon a taxi. When arriving at airports, avoid the touts who immediately surround you, and head instead to the taxi rank outside where you are less likely to be overcharged.

A taxi ride in Macau costs upwards of MOP$19, but the place is small and final fares mostly amount to MOP$60–70. Meter-run taxis are inexpensive in Shenzhen and Guangzhou.

Note that tipping the driver is not expected in Hong Kong, Shenzhen, Macau and Guangzhou.

Ferries

Travelling by ferry is a scenic way to see Hong Kong, with beautiful harbour views along the water. A large number of vessels ply between Hong Kong and Macau, many of which are high-speed and operate round the clock. The most celebrated is the **Star Ferry** across Victoria Harbour, which has been taking passengers between Hong Kong Island and Kowloon for over a century and offers views of both sides of the harbour. Fares vary depending on whether you sit on the upper or lower deck, and if you travel on a weekend (weekdays are cheaper).

As well as the Star Ferry, **First Ferries** run services to Lantau, Lamma and Cheung Chau islands from the outlying islands ferry terminal in Central. **Hong Kong and Kowloon Ferry** operates from Central to Lamma and Peng Chau, while **Tsui Wah Ferry** serves Po Toi Island and Lamma from Hong Kong Island's south coast. Octopus cards are valid on most ferries.

Driving

Renting a car in Hong Kong is not advised; the paperwork required to obtain a Chinese driving licence is extensive. Many locals don't drive at all, since public transport offers a quick and cheap way to get to any destination, and nothing is ever too far away. Parking is also notoriously difficult in Hong Kong. Roads in Macau can also be narrow and difficult to drive down.

If you are set on driving, however, rental agencies such as **Avis** and **Hertz** have branches in Hong Kong. Overseas driving licences are valid in Hong Kong for visitors staying for fewer than 12 months. You will also need an International Driving Permit. Most rental companies require you to be a minimum age of 21 and some apply young driver surcharges for under 25s.

Rules of the Road

The speed limit in Hong Kong is 50 km/h (31 mph approx); outside of the city, it's usually 70 km/h (43 mph approx). The blood-alcohol concentration (BAC) is 0.05 percent and is strictly enforced.

Note that there are rules pertaining to crossing the Hong Kong border into China. If you need to drive across the boundary, you will need to apply for licenses and permits. Information and forms can be found on the Hong Kong SAR Government website (see p145).

Cycling

With their picturesque waterfronts, unspoiled greenery and urban centres, Hong Kong, Macau and Shenzhen are a joy to cycle around.

Each city is home to specific cycling routes and promenades, too, including challenging road bike trails.

In Hong Kong, many visitors choose to cycle in the New Territories and outlying islands, since they are less congested and provide lush seaside views along the way. Bikes are easy to rent, and you can find a list of shops offering rentals across the city on the **Hong Kong Cycling Alliance** website. Once you're on two wheels, always wear a helmet, ride on cycle tracks and networks and follow the same rules that apply to drivers when cycling on roads. The **Cycling Information Centre (CIC)** is an online platform with further information on the likes of regulations, cycling tracks and traffic signs in Hong Kong.

Cycling in Macau is just as much a leisurely experience. Taipa Island tends to have the most favoured cycle routes, with many bikes available to hire near Pak Tai Temple. In Shenzhen, meanwhile, many of the hilly routes require a mountain bike and can prove difficult, requiring a good level of fitness.

Walking

Hong Kong is one of the best cities to walk in, with many streets being either fully or part pedestrianized, and drivers giving way to pedestrians. Elevated walkways in the Central District connect shops, offices and hotels, and clear signs direct visitors to tourist landmarks, meaning it's difficult to lose your bearings.

Many walking tours also operate in the city. **Guided walks** by Walk Hong Kong and Jason Wordie are good for all levels, exploring Hong Kong's architecture, heritage, wildlife and countryside. Hundreds of kilometres of hiking trails also weave across the city. Many are run by the **Agriculture, Fisheries and Conservation Department (AFCD)**.

Macau, Guangzhou and Shenzhen are very walkable, too. Macau's old town is compact, though its narrow alleys can get crowded very quickly. Shenzhen is great for hiking, with mountain trails for every level.

Guided Tours

Many guided bus, coach and boat tours operate in Hong Kong and its surrounding areas, and can be a great way of seeing the sights. The **China Travel Service** (CTS) can organize visas, tours and packages to Macau and mainland China. **Splendid Tours** specializes in excursions around Hong Kong, Macau, Shenzhen and Guangzhou. Package coach tours covering the region can be booked through **Gray Line Tours**. Explore the coast with day and night harbour cruises, some with drinks, either on Star Ferry's harbour tour or aboard the **Aqua Luna** wooden junk. Various companies also offer **junks** for private charter around Hong Kong's many islands.

Practical Information

Passports and Visas

For entry requirements, including visas, consult your nearest Hong Kong embassy or check the **Hong Kong SAR Government** website. Citizens of the US, Canada, Australia, New Zealand and most European countries only need a valid passport to enter Hong Kong for a stay of up to 90 days; UK passport holders – valid for at least one month after you intend to leave – can stay 180 days. Visitors from the US, Canada and Australia may stay in Macau for at least 30 days without a visa; citizens of the European Union are allowed to stay 90 days, and UK nationals can stay for up to six months. All other visitors are advised to contact their local Chinese embassy for visa requirements.

All foreign nationals require a **visa** to enter mainland China; these should be obtained through the **China Travel Service** in Hong Kong, or Chinese embassies and consulates in your own country. Visa regulations can change, so always make sure to check the requirements.

Five-day visas for Shenzhen (¥168-304 depending on nationality) are available at Shekou Port, Huanggang Port, Shenzhen Airport and the Lo Wu (Luo Hu) crossing, but not at Futian. A 72-hour transit visa is available at Guangzhou airport for those arriving on international flights who have proof of onward air travel to a third country (so you can't be on a round-trip from Hong Kong). Do not attempt to travel beyond the visa's permitted area, and check the latest information before travelling.

Government Advice

Now more than ever, it is important to consult both your and the Hong Kong government's advice before travelling. The **UK Foreign and Commonwealth Office**, the **US State Department**, the **Australian Department of Foreign Affairs and Trade** and the Hong Kong SAR Government offer the latest information on security, health and local regulations.

Customs Information

You can find information on the laws relating to goods and currency taken in or out of Hong Kong on the **Hong Kong Tourism Board (HKTB)** website and Macau on the **Macao Customs Service** website. For information on China more generally, visit the **General Administration of Customs People's Republic of China** website.

Hong Kong and Macau are free ports and only levy customs duties on spirits and tobacco. Visitors over 18 years old are allowed to import 1 litre of spirits of 30% ABV or higher (no limit on alcohol less than 30%); plus 25g of tobacco products.

Visitors to China can import 200 cigarettes or 20 cigars or 250g of tobacco, plus 1.5 litres of alcoholic beverages over 12% ABV, and up to the equivalent of US$5000 in foreign currency. You cannot export anything of cultural importance (this may apply to antiques), nor any endangered animal or plant products.

Insurance

We recommend that you take out a comprehensive insurance policy covering theft, loss of belongings, medical care, cancellations and delays, and read the small print carefully.

Health

Hong Kong has an excellent healthcare system. There is no free health care for visitors, so payment of medical expenses is the patient's responsibility. You'll have to recoup the costs for any consultations, treatment and prescriptions through your travel insurance policy; it is therefore important to arrange comprehensive travel insurance before travelling. There are hospitals, clinics and dentists across the region with English-speaking staff.

Pollution is a major health issue. Poor air quality, tropical humidity and crowded conditions contribute to the spread of respiratory complaints. Tap water is best avoided, and locally caught seafood is unsafe to eat (most restaurants import theirs).

Seawater quality varies, and toxic algal blooms

can make swimming ill-advised. Rare shark sightings off Hong Kong cause panic; stick to beaches that are netted and well patrolled. Summer days can get very hot; carry a bottle of water and avoid too much activity during the hottest part of the day. Wear cool, light, loose cotton clothing, with a hat. In winter, when temperatures can drop below 20ºC, bring along a light sweater as well as a waterproof jacket.

For information regarding COVID-19 vaccination requirements, consult government advice *(see p144)*. No other vaccinations are required for Hong Kong, Macau or China, except for yellow fever if you're coming from an area where the disease is endemic.

Smoking, Alcohol and Drugs

Smoking is banned in public places. A tough line is taken on illegal drugs; if convicted you can face time in prison, and China has executed foreign nationals for drug trafficking. Hong Kong has a strict limit of 0.05 per cent BAC (blood alcohol concentration) for drivers.

ID

By law you must carry identification with you at all times in Hong Kong and its surrounding areas. A photocopy of your passport photo page and visa should suffice. It is an offence to fail to show proof of identity if stopped by a police officer.

Personal Security

Hong Kong is generally a safe place to visit, but like most cities, petty crime does take place. Keep a close hold on personal possessions, using a hotel safe if provided. Be careful crossing the road; traffic rules are ignored by many and accidents involving pedestrians are common.

In the event of a crime or a crisis, various helplines are available. Call the **Guangzhou and Shenzhen fire, ambulance and police** emergency number if you need urgent services in China. In **Hong Kong and Macau fire, ambulance and police** services can be contacted from a mobile or landline. Give your location, details about the problem and a telephone number. For less pressing matters, it is advisable to contact the local police stations. Hong Kong police wear blue uniforms; many speak English or will call for assistance if they don't. Chinese police officers also wear blue uniforms but are unlikely to be bilingual.

Homosexuality was decriminalized in Hong Kong in 1991, but there is still a long way to go when it comes to LGBTQ+ rights. Same-sex marriage is not legalized, and while the right to change your gender is legal, it requires surgery to be made official. China is a highly conservative society, with homosexuality largely disapproved of and mis-understood; as such, in some parts of Hong Kong, overt displays of affection may receive a negative response from locals. Young locals are generally more accepting, and Hong Kong has a good LGBTQ+ scene, with many gay clubs and pride events.

DIRECTORY

PASSPORTS AND VISAS

China Travel Service
W ctshk.com

Hong Kong SAR Government
W gov.hk

Visa
W immd.gov.hk
W fsm.gov.mo/psp/eng/EDoN.html
W visaforchina.org

GOVERNMENT ADVICE

Australian Department of Foreign Affairs and Trade
W dfat.gov.au

UK Foreign and Commonwealth Office
W gov.uk/foreign-travel-advice

US State Department
W travel.state.gov

CUSTOMS INFORMATION

General Administration of Customs People's Republic of China
W english.customs.gov.cn

Hong Kong Tourism Board (HKTB)
W discoverhongkong.com

Macao Customs Service
W customs.gov.mo

PERSONAL SECURITY

Guangzhou and Shenzhen fire, ambulance and police
C 119, 120, 110

Hong Kong and Macau fire, ambulance and police
C 999

Travellers with Specific Requirements

Hong Kong has a wide range of facilities for people with specific requirements. All MTR stations have tacticle guide paths, induction loops at their information centres, and step-free access; staff are always on hand to assist visually and hearing impaired passengers, and those with reduced mobility. Buses, taxis, ferries and trams are also adaptable for those with specific requirements.

The Hong Kong Tourism Board (HKTB) website (see p145) has an informative "Accessible Hong Kong" section, and also offers information about facilities in Macau, Shenzhen and Guangzhou, though these are limited. The **Hong Kong Society for Rehabilitation** also lists accessible attractions in the city, such as hotels, shops and restaurants.

Time Zone

Hong Kong, Macau and China are 8 hours ahead of Greenwich Mean Time and 13 hours ahead of US Eastern Standard Time.

Money

Local currencies are the Hong Kong dollar (HK$), the pataca (MOP$) in Macau and the Chinese yuan (¥RMB). The ¥RMB is worth more than the HK$, which in turn is worth fractionally more than the MOP$. HK$ are accepted in Macau but ¥RMB are needed for mainland China.

As it's one of the world's financial hubs, you're rarely far away from a bank or an ATM in Hong Kong, and they are similarly common in Macau and China. Credit and debit cards are widely accepted by ATMs, and in hotels, restaurants and shops that see plenty of foreign custom, but at smaller businesses you'll need cash. Both banks and money exchangers (which are only plentiful in the downtown areas of Hong Kong) often give poor exchange rates compared with using an ATM – check exchange rates online or check with your own bank about any transaction fees. In an emergency, money can be wired through local banks or **Western Union**.

Tipping is not the done thing in Hong Kong, though it is appreciated.

Electrical Appliances

Mains electricity in Hong Kong, Macau and China runs at 220V, 50Hz, so North American electrical devices will need converters. Plugs are British-style three square pins in Hong Kong but two round pins in Macau and China, though many Chinese sockets are universal. Adapters are sold at street stalls.

Mobile Phones and Wi-Fi

Depending on your mobile phone provider, roaming rates can be expensive in Hong Kong and Macau; check with your phone company before travel. A cheaper option is to get a local SIM card.

Several local companies sell local pay-as-you-go SIM cards, though none is better-value than the **Discover Hong Kong Tourist SIM Card**, which is available from the 1010 outlet at the airport, tourist offices and convenience stores across the city. A Hong Kong SIM card may work in China; if not, buy a Chinese one from any China Mobile shop or street kiosk, and top it up with a chongzhi ka (prepaid card).

Hong Kong is well-connected to the internet, with fast, free Wi-Fi available at the airport and most cafés and public parks. Hong Kong Central Library, an enormous complex in Causeway Bay, has both free Wi-Fi and hundreds of desktop terminals. In Macau, Wi-Fi is not as widespread, but there are free terminals at the tourist office in Largo do Senado.

In China, expect news and social media sites, such as Facebook and Twitter, to be blocked unless you have a VPN.

Postal Services

The Hong Kong postal service is rapid and efficient. Local mail takes one to two days. Zone 1 air mail (all of Asia except Japan) takes three to five days. Zone 2 (the rest of the world) takes five to seven days. The **General Post Office** operates a poste restante service.

The Chinese postal service is fairly fast and efficient, although overseas rates are pricey and sending parcels can be tedious. Be warned that International Express Mail (EMS) is unreliable.

Weather

Set just inside the tropics, Hong Kong, Macau and southern China share the same weather pattern. Summers (June–Sep) are very hot and dry with temperatures around 86 °F (30 °C) and typhoons that bring destructive winds and heavy rainfall; flights and ferries can be cancelled at short notice. Winters (Dec–Mar) are relatively cool and dry, with daytime temperatures sometimes as low as 59 °F (15 °C).

Opening Hours

Hong Kong's office hours are 9am–5pm Mon–Fri (till 12:30pm Sat). Most shops open daily but not usually before 10am, staying open until 7pm or later. Official hours in Macau are Mon–Fri 9am–1pm and 3pm–5pm, and 9am–1pm Sat. China's opening times are 9am–5pm Mon–Fri for banks and offices, with some opening through the weekend too, though with reduced services (banks might not offer foreign exchange). Shops in China open early and close late.

Across the region, everything closes for the first three days of the Chinese New Year (late Jan or early Feb), with reduced hours for the rest of the two-week-long festival. Other days when you might find government offices and businesses shut are New Year's Day (1 Jan), Qingming (4 or 5 Apr), May Day (1 May), the Dragon Boat Festival (late May or Jun), the Mid-Autumn Festival (late Sep) and National Day (1–3 Oct, China only).

COVID-19 Increased rates of infection may result in temporary opening hours and/or closures. Always check ahead before visiting museums, attractions and hospitality venues.

Visitor Information

The Hong Kong Tourism Board (HKTB) (see p145) has booths at major entry points to the city, and two branches (8am–8pm daily).

The **Macau Government Tourist Office** is situated on the west side of Largo do Senado (9am– 6pm daily) as well as at all air, land and sea entry points.

Language

The Hong Kong region is primarily Cantonese-speaking. Mandarin Chinese is the official language of education and business English is spoken and used on signage in the city, though less so in the New Territories.

A decreasing number of people speak Portuguese in Macau. In Shenzhen and Guangzhou, street signs are in English, but you'll need a phrasebook to get far on your own.

Taxes and Refunds

Hong Kong is a tax-free destination, with no sales taxes on any goods.

Accommodation

In Hong Kong, expect to pay a premium for space. A 3 percent government tax and a 10 percent service charge will be added to most bills.

There are two central **YHA (Hong Kong)** youth hostels in Hong Kong. Check **YHA China** for hostels elsewhere. Good rooms, facilities and higher prices are offered by various churches and international organizations such as the **YMCA**.

Hotels range from basic business models to some of the world's best. Macau and Shenzhen have a good range of hotels with prices lower than in Hong Kong. **Agoda** and **CTrip** are great websites to book accommodation online.

Places to Stay

PRICE CATEGORIES

For a standard, double room per night (with breakfast if included), taxes and extra charges.

$ under HK$1,000 $$ HK$1,000–2,500 $$$ over HK$2,500
¥ under ¥400   ¥¥ ¥400–1000   ¥¥¥ over ¥1000

Luxury Hotels

Kerry Hotel

MAP R3 ■ 38 Hung Luen Rd, Hung Hom, Kowloon ■ 2252 5888 ■ www.shangri-la.com/en/hongkong/kerry ■ $$$

Run by the Shangri-La Hotels and Resorts group, Kerry Hotel has spacious rooms with captivating views of Victoria Harbour from the Kowloon side. Don't leave without taking a dip in the infinity pool.

The Langham

MAP M4 ■ 8 Peking Rd, Tsim Sha Tsui, Kowloon ■ 2375 1133 ■ www.langhamhotels.com ■ $$

Restrained opulence reigns throughout. There is a good gym, pool and sauna, and many top-quality restaurants, including the impressive two-Michelin-starred T'ang Court, which is decked out like a Mongolian tent.

Banyan Tree Macau

Galaxy Macau Resort, Avenida Marginal Flor de Lotus, Cotai Strip ■ 8883 6888 ■ www.banyantree.com/en/macau ■ $$$

With great views of Macau's skyline, this magnificent resort hotel is supremely luxurious in style and amenities. Both the award-winning restaurants and the Southeast Asian-themed spa are of the highest quality.

Conrad

MAP M6 ■ 88 Queensway, Admiralty ■ 2894 8888 ■ www.conradhotels3.hilton.com ■ $$$

This stylish hotel offers rooms with superb views of the city from the 61st floor of Pacific Place. A hotel immersed in luxury, your every need is catered for at the Conrad.

Garden Hotel Guangzhou

368 Huangshi Dong Lu, Guangzhou ■ 8333 8989 ■ www.gardenhotel.com ■ ¥¥¥

The cavernous lobby gives a sense of the size of this imposing 1,000-plus room five-star hotel, boasting its own upmarket shopping mall and good eating options. Prices are inclusive of limousine transfers.

The Grand Hyatt

MAP N5 ■ 1 Harbour Rd, Wan Chai ■ 2588 1234 ■ www.hyatt.com ■ $$$

Next to the Convention Centre and the premier choice for unbridled luxury in Wan Chai, the Grand Hyatt has looked after high-profile guests including former US President Bill Clinton. Rooms have a modern feel, and include all the high-tech mod-cons.

House 1881

MAP M4 ■ 2A Canton Rd, Tsim Sha Tsui ■ 3988 0000 ■ www.house1881.com ■ $$$

The blend of superb colonial architecture and contemporary interiors makes this Hong Kong's top boutique hotel. Located in the beautiful former headquarters of the Marine Police, there are ten exquisitely designed suites with superb facilities as well as a fabulous stone terrace overlooking the Heritage 1881 courtyard.

Island Shangri-La

MAP M6 ■ Pacific Place, Central ■ 2877 3838 ■ www.shangri-la.com ■ $$$

The grandiose lobby, huge chandeliers and stunning mural adorning the atrium are a prelude to the elegantly decorated rooms, with terrific Peak or harbour views.

The Landmark Mandarin Oriental

MAP L5 ■ 15 Queen's Rd Central ■ 2132 0188 ■ www.mandarinoriental.com ■ $$$

A stylish conversion of former offices has created some of the largest rooms in Asia, all with circular sunken baths, HD TVs and Wi-Fi. The two-floor luxury spa is one of the city's best.

The Mandarin Oriental HK

MAP K4 ■ 5 Connaught Rd, Central ■ 2522 0111 ■ www.mandarinoriental.com ■ $$$

In an excellent location in the heart of the financial

district, this fashionable hotel overlooks Victoria Harbour. The bustling public areas are one of the territory's most popular meeting places, while the rooms have an elegant atmosphere and a modern, luxurious design, which incorporates every high-tech convenience possible.

The Peninsula
MAP N4 ▪ Salisbury Rd, Kowloon ▪ 2920 2888 ▪ www.peninsula.com ▪ $$$

Hong Kong's original luxury offering opened in 1928 and is still one of the city's best-loved hotels. Overlooking Victoria Harbour, the Neo-Classical Peninsula (see p85) is famous for restrained luxury and excellent service.

Ritz-Carlton, Guangzhou
MAP L2 ▪ 3 Xing An Rd, Guangzhou ▪ 3813 6688 ▪ www.ritzcarlton.com ▪ ¥¥¥

One of the city's finest luxury hotels is located in Pearl River City opposite the Guangzhou Tower. Experience luxury and indulge yourself in classic Ritz-Carlton service.

Ritz-Carlton, Hong Kong
MAP L2 ▪ International Commerce Centre, 1 Austin Rd W, Kowloon ▪ 2263 2263 ▪ www.ritzcarlton.com ▪ $$$

The views are incredible from Hong Kong's tallest building. The quality of design and in-room technology make it the epitome of modern luxury. It also features the "highest bar in the world".

Shangri-La Hotel Shenzhen
MAP D1 ▪ Jianshe Lu, Shenzhen ▪ 8233 0888 ▪ www.shangri-la.com ▪ ¥¥¥

Close to the main shopping areas and railway station, the Shangri-la makes a wonderful escape from Shenzhen's seething retail madness. The rooftop pool is perfect for relaxing.

The Upper House
MAP M4 ▪ Pacific Place, 88 Queensway, Central ▪ 2918 1838 ▪ www.upperhouse.com ▪ $$$

This hotel has beautifully styled rooms with superb views and great facilities. Café Gray Deluxe restaurant and lounge on the 49th floor is a regular watering hole for Hong Kong's fashionable set.

The Venetian
Estrada da Baía de N Senhora da Esperança, Taipa, Macau ▪ 2882 8888 ▪ www.venetianmacao.com ▪ $$$

Macau's most spectacular resort-casino is a recreation of the Las Vegas dream of Italy, but with sampans among the gondolas. The megaresort is suites only, and has a themed shopping mall designed to look like the canals of Venice, a 1,800-seat theatre and all the dining options you could want.

Mid-Range Hotels in Hong Kong

The Eaton Hotel
MAP N1 ▪ 380 Nathan Rd ▪ 2782 1818 ▪ www.eaton-hotel.com ▪ $$

The best option in the Yau Ma Tei and Jordan area. At The Eaton,

rooms are smart and the lobby offers a flood of natural light, outdoor seating as well as an oasis of greenery.

Empire Hotel Kowloon
MAP N3 ▪ 62 Kimberley Rd, Tsim Sha Tsui ▪ 3692 2222 ▪ www.empirehotel.com.hk ▪ $$

This very smart hotel with a modern gym and a lovely atrium pool is a complete contrast to its threadbare sister in Wan Chai. Rooms are equipped with the latest internet and audiovisual gadgetry. The location is perfect for Tsim Sha Tsui shopping and dining.

Hyatt Regency
MAP N4 ▪ 18 Hanoi Rd, Tsim Sha Tsui ▪ 2311 1234 ▪ www.hyatt.com ▪ $$

Located in one of Kowloon's tallest towers, this impressive hotel is aimed at both business as well as leisure travellers. Rooms on the upper floors boast exceptional views of Hong Kong and the hotel provides a great location for all the attractions on offer around Kowloon.

The Luxe Manor
MAP N3 ▪ 39 Kimberley Rd, Tsim Sha Tsui ▪ 3763 8888 ▪ www.theluxemanor.com ▪ $$

A stylish boutique hotel located in Kowloon, The Luxe Manor combines eclectic, almost surreal, decor with high-tech features. The rooms are decorated with painted picture frames, which climb the walls onto the ceiling and other funky touches.

The Mira
MAP N3 ▪ 118 Nathan Rd, Tsim Sha Tsui ▪ 2368 1111 ▪ www.themira hotel.com ▪ $$

The Mira is chic, slick, futuristic and mini-malistic; however you cannot help admiring the redesign of this well-maintained business hotel. The hydro pool and luxury spa are definite attractions.

Regal Airport Hotel
MAP B5 ▪ 9 Cheong Tat Rd, Chek Lap Kok ▪ 2286 8888 ▪ www.regalhotel. com ▪ $$

Hong Kong's largest hotel links directly to the airport terminal and features large rooms with avant-garde interior designs. Seven restaurants and bars provide a plethora of cuisine choices.

OZO Wesley Hong Kong
MAP N6 ▪ 22 Hennessy Rd, Wan Chai ▪ 2292 3000 ▪ www.ozohotels.com ▪ $$

Comfortable beds in modern rooms with city views and a central location make this a good choice on the island. Also has a small gym and high tech check-in and information screens in the lobby.

Mid-Range Hotels in Macau & China

Ole Tai Sam Un Hotel
43–45 Rua da Caldeira, Macau ▪ 2893 8818 ▪ oletaisamunhotel. com ▪ $

Located close to Macau's historic centre, this hotel offers well-equipped, modern rooms with hardwood floors and tasteful decor. The breakfast buffet includes a good variety of options. Senado Square is a 10-minute walk away.

Best Western Shenzhen Felicity Hotel
1085 Heping Lu, Shenzhen ▪ 2558 6333 ▪ www.bwsz.net ▪ ¥¥

This good-value hotel is reasonably well located and even boasts its own art gallery. Standards are high and guests can take advantage of the three restaurants as well as the gym, pool and sauna. On-line bookings are cheaper.

Crowne Plaza Hotel and Suites Landmark, Shenzhen
3018 Nanhu Lu, Shenzhen ▪ 8217 2288 ▪ www.ihg.com ▪ ¥¥

Close to the railway station, this hotel offers lovely rooms and exten-sive facilities, including a fitness centre, a gym and indoor pool.

Guangdong Victory Hotel
53 Shamian Bei Jie, Guangzhou ▪ 8121 6688 ▪ www.guangdong victoryhotel.com ▪ ¥¥

Formerly the Victoria Hotel, this hotel occupies two sites on Shamian Island – the main Neo-Classical block and the original colonial building. Facilities include several restaurants, a swimming pool and a sauna.

Holiday Inn
82–86 Rua de Pequim, Macau ▪ 2878 3333 ▪ www.holidayinn. com ▪ $$

Set close to Lisboa's many casinos and convenient for central Macau. Rooms (with cable TV) are simply furnished but there's a good range of facilities, including gym, pool, sauna and a decent restaurant for Cantonese and Szechuan food.

Hotel Royal Macau
Estrada da Vitoria 2–4, Macau ▪ 2855 2222 ▪ www.hotelroyal.com. mo ▪ $$

The Hotel Royal is one of Macau's oldest hotels. It was refurbished with modern amenities. It features an indoor pool, gym and sauna. It's also close to the heart of town and within sight of the pretty Guia Lighthouse.

The Panglin Hotel
2002 Jiabin Lu, Lowu, Shenzhen ▪ 2518 5888 ▪ www.panglin-hotel. com ▪ ¥¥

Smart and modern, this is one of Shenzhen's superior hotels, about 4 km (2 miles) from the railway station. Rooms are decent and have cable TV. Services include station shuttle bus, baby-sitting and 24-hour room service. Numerous dining options; Sky Paradise buffet on the 50th floor is Shenzhen's highest revolving restaurant.

Value-for-Money Hotels

2 Macdonnell Road
MAP K6 ▪ 2 Macdonnell Rd, Central ▪ 2132 2132 ▪ www.twomr.com.hk ▪ $$

With pleasant rooms, a good Central location and excellent views across the Zoological and Botanical Gardens to the city and harbour, Macdonnell Road offers good value apartments. Turnover service, use of gym, satellite and cable TV, kitchenette and Central shuttle bus are all included in the price. Cots for children and babysitting services are offered. Long-stay packages also available.

Booth Lodge
MAP N1 ▪ 11 Wing Sing Lane, Yau Ma Tei, Kowloon ▪ 2771 9266 ▪ www.salvationarmy.org.hk/en/services/booth ▪ $$
Air-conditioned rooms with a shower, bath, fridge, phone and TV are adequate, and the location and prices are great at this Salvation Army-run hotel.

Caritas Bianchi Lodge
MAP N1 ▪ 4 Cliff Rd, Yau Ma Tei, Kowloon ▪ 2388 1111 ▪ www.caritas-chs.org.hk ▪ $$
Like Booth Lodge next door, there's only a chapel and restaurant-cum-café to amuse you here. Still, the rooms are large by any standards. The hotel is run by the Social Welfare Bureau of the Roman Catholic Church.

The Empire Hotel
MAP N6 ▪ 33 Hennessy Rd, Wan Chai ▪ 3692 2111 ▪ www.empirehotel.com.hk ▪ $$
Marooned between the area's two main roads, the Empire is right in the heart of Wan Chai so you're paying for location rather than luxury. The prices are competitive, the service is decent and there's a rooftop pool, plus a gym as well as a pleasant restaurant in the lobby.

The Harbourview
MAP N5 ▪ 4 Harbour Rd, Wan Chai ▪ 2911 1358 ▪ www.theharbourview.com.hk ▪ $$
This modern Chinese YMCA-run hotel charges a premium for the location, but low-season discounts are available. Rooms are comfortable and well-appointed. Two restaurants and a gym.

Rosedale on the Park
MAP Q6 ▪ 8 Shelter St, Causeway Bay ▪ 2127 8888 ▪ hongkong.rosedalehotels.com ▪ $$
This self-styled "cyber boutique hotel" offers reasonable value overlooking Victoria Park. The look is sleek and modern. The rooms are small but well laid-out and there is a range of business services.

The Salisbury YMCA
MAP M4 ▪ 41 Salisbury Rd, Tsim Sha Tsui ▪ 2268 7000 ▪ www.ymcahk.org.hk ▪ $$
Don't be put off by the initials. For value, views and location, the always-popular YMCA, next door to the posh Peninsula, can't be beaten. The well-furnished rooms are spacious, equipped with laptop ports, and satellite and cable TV. A swimming pool, sauna, gym and an indoor climbing wall round off the facilities. Family suites are terrific.

The Wharney
MAP N6 ▪ 57–73 Lockhart Rd, Wan Chai ▪ 2861 1000 ▪ www.wharney.com ▪ $$
Right in the increasingly smart centre of Wan Chai, the Wharney offers decent surroundings, a revamped gym and pool, sauna, business centre and a couple of restaurants. Rooms are well-appointed but a bit small.

Budget Accommodation

BP International House
MAP M2 ▪ 8 Austin Rd, Tsim Sha Tsui ▪ 2376 1111 ▪ www.bpih.com.hk ▪ $
The boxy rooms with vintage wallpaper have smallish beds, but the place is clean, efficient and can be cheap, and has lovely views over Kowloon Park.

Bradbury Hall Hostel
MAP F3 ▪ Chek Keng, Sai Kung, New Territories ▪ 2328 2458 ▪ www.yha.org.hk ▪ $
As you might expect from its remote location, the Bradbury Hall Hostel has basic, barrack-like dorms. Those with tents may want to walk on and pitch camp at Tai Long Wan's lovely beaches nearby.

Bradbury Jockey Club Youth Hostel
MAP F2 ▪ 66 Tai Mei Tuk, New Territories ▪ 2662 5123 ▪ www.yha.org.hk ▪ $
Located by the reservoir, Bradbury Jockey Club Youth Hostel is pleasant and it makes for a good base or stop-off for walkers exploring the beautiful Plover Cove area. Air-conditioned singles, doubles or dorms are available.

For a key to hotel price categories see p148

Chungking House, Chungking Mansions

MAP N4 ▪ Block 4A/5F, 40 Nathan Rd, Tsim Sha Tsui ▪ 2739 1600 ▪ www. chungkinghouse.com ▪ $

Staying at the mansions is popular with some budget travellers but not so with others (see p87). The dingy hallways lead to dozens of guesthouses offering cheap accommodation in an excellent location. Oppressive but fascinating, this is Hong Kong's cultural melting pot. Chungking House has large rooms and is a great option.

Holy Carpenter Guest House

MAP R2 ▪ 1 Dyer Ave, Hung Hom, Kowloon ▪ 2362 0301 ▪ www. holycarpenter.org.hk/ holyHotel ▪ $

Run by the Sheng Kung Hui Holy Carpenter Church, this is a pleasant guesthouse. Facilities in double and triple rooms are basic but include TV, phone, bathroom, shower and air conditioning.

Homy Hotel Central

MAP K4 ▪ 157 Wing Lok St, Sheung Wan ▪ 8100 0189 ▪ www. homyinn.com.hk ▪ $

This three-star hotel, near the Sheung Wan MTR station, is a few minutes away from Soho and other landmarks in Central. Rooms are clean and modest in size.

Sze Lok Yuen Hostel

MAP D3 ▪ Tai Mo Shan, Tsuen Wan, New Territories ▪ 2488 8188 ▪ www.yha.org.hk ▪ $

A basic hikers' crash-pad, Sze Lok Yuen is close to the summit of Tai Mo Shan, Hong Kong's tallest peak. The views of the surrounding mountains are spectacular, but its dorm rooms have no fans or air conditioning. The altitude cools things down though in all but the hottest months. Camping is also permitted here.

YHA Mei Ho House Youth Hostel

MAP M1 ▪ Block 41, Shek Kip Mei Estate, Sham Shui Po, Kowloon ▪ 3728 3500 ▪ www. yha.org.hk ▪ $

A fully renovated public resettlement block from 1954, this hostel has en-suite air-conditioned doubles, family rooms and dorms. There is an on-site store, café, shared kitchen and laundry.

Long-Stay Hotels

The Bay Bridge

MAP D3 ▪ 123 Castle Peak Rd, Yau Kom Tau, Tsuen Wan, Kowloon ▪ 2945 1111 ▪ www. baybridgehongkong. com ▪ HK$27,000– HK$66,000 per month

Given the Tseun Wan location, these smart studio and suite apartments are not for those who must be at the centre of things. Facilities include a gym and outdoor pool.

Chi Residences

MAP J4 ▪ 138 Connaught Rd W, Sai Ying Pun ▪ 3443 6888 ▪ www. chi-residences.com ▪ HK$23,000–HK$62,000 per month

The beautifully appointed rooms here are decorated in a contemporary style and offer views of Victoria Harbour. Chi Residences manage several properties in other locations in Hong Kong.

Harbourfront Horizon Suites

MAP Q3 ▪ 8 Hung Luen Rd, Hung Hom Bay, Kowloon ▪ 3157 8888 ▪ www.horizonhotels. com.hk ▪ HK$19,800– HK$35,000 per month

Located a stone's throw away from Hung Hom MTR station and within walking distance of Tsim Sha Tsui, Harbourfront Horizon Suites features modern and bright two- and three-bedroom apartments overlooking Victoria Bay. Beautiful gardens, a swimming pool as well as a fitness centre are available at the complex.

Ovolo Central

MAP J5 ▪ 2 Arbuthnot Rd ▪ 3755 3000 ▪ www. ovolohotels.com ▪ HK$66,000 per month

These swanky modern residences are well-located close to the heart of Central. They have all the facilities of a deluxe hotel, including free high-speed Wi-Fi, Apple TV as well as fun gaming consoles for a bit of relaxation.

Shama Central

MAP K5 ▪ 26 Peel St, Central ▪ MAP K5 ▪ 2103 1713 ▪ www. shama.com ▪ HK$42,000– HK$59,700 per month

Centrally located above a bustling produce market, this modern block offers cosy studios and spacious apartments with smart furnishings, daily maid service, Wi-Fi internet access, self-service laundry and kitchenettes.

YesInn
MAP N1 ▪ 2/F, 1B, Wing Sing Lane, Yau Ma Tei, Kowloon ▪ 3427 6000 ▪ www.yesinn.com ▪ HK$5270–HK$9820 per month
Bright and small, YesInn is located near the Temple Street Night Market. Featuring inexpensive serviced en-suite double rooms and dorms with shared kitchens, this is a great option for long term rental.

Great Escapes

Harbour Plaza Resort City
MAP C2 ▪ 18 Tin Yan Rd, Tin Shui Wai, New Territories ▪ 2180 6688 ▪ www.harbour-plaza.com ▪ $
In the New Territories, this extensive resort complex offers a vast array of sports and recreation facilities, including cinemas, shops, gyms, sports tracks and courts, Chinese and international restaurants, and nearby historical and beauty spots. All rooms include the basics with a small lounge area.

Jockey Club Mount Davis Youth Hostel
MAP E5 ▪ Mount Davis Path, Kennedy Town ▪ 2817 5715 ▪ www.yha.org.hk ▪ $
A popular budget option for the more adventurous, this lovely and friendly hostel sits atop Mount Davis at the western edge of Hong Kong Island. The surroundings are peaceful and beautiful, and the staff are helpful. This hostel is a little out of the way so you may need to take a taxi there.

SanVa
65–67 Rua da Felicidade, Macau ▪ www.sanvahotel.com ▪ No credit cards ▪ $
Step back in time with this genuine 1920s guesthouse. Rooms have ceiling fans and wash basin, and all other facilities are shared. SanVa is clean, romantic and lovingly run.

Grand Coloane Resort
Estrada de Hac Sa 1918, Ilha de Coloane, Macau ▪ 2887 1111 ▪ www.grandcoloane.com ▪ $$
All rooms come with their own terrace and sea views. There's a small sandy beach and an 18-hole golf course. You can also practise your swing on the ocean driving range with balls that float.

Hong Kong Gold Coast Hotel
MAP B3 ▪ 1 Castle Peak Rd, Kowloon ▪ 2452 8888 ▪ www.sino-hotels.com/hk/gold-coast ▪ $$
This fine resort offers sea views from its well-equipped rooms. The accommodation complex is unlovely from outside, but recreation facilities include pool, pitch-and-putt golf course, tennis courts and running track.

Pousada de Coloane
Praia de Cheoc-Van, Coloane Island, Macau ▪ 2888 2143 ▪ www.hotelpcoloane.com.mo ▪ $$
This tiny, remote hotel lies at the far end of Coloane, overlooking a small, pretty beach. It boasts a nice swimming pool, deck area and a Portuguese-style restaurant and bar. Room fittings are decent and well equipped.

Rocks Hotel
Fisherman's Wharf, Avenida Dr Sun Yat-Sen, Macau ▪ 2878 2782 ▪ www.rockshotel.com.mo ▪ $$
Set above the Fisherman's Wharf shopping area, this is a Victorian-style place. The period rooms here are equipped with modern amenities and command pretty sea views. As an added element, the staff dress in historical clothing.

The Warwick
MAP C6 ▪ East Bay, Cheung Chau ▪ 2981 0081 ▪ $$
An affordable alternative to city living, magical Cheung Chau's only major hotel offers fine sea views next to good beaches with windsurf and kayak hire. Great coastal walks are around the headland. The exterior is 1960s municipal.

Tai O Heritage Hotel
MAP A5 ▪ Shek Tsai Po St, Tai O, Lantau Island ▪ 2985 8383 ▪ www.taioheritagehotel.com ▪ $$$
Housed in an 110-year-old former colonial police station, this beautiful hotel is the perfect base from which to explore the sleepy fishing town on Tai O and Lantau Island beyond. The five rooms and four suites are all individually decorated in an elegant, colonial style.

White Swan Hotel
1 Southern St, Shamian Island, Guangzhou ▪ 8188 6968 ▪ www.whiteswanhotel.com ▪ ¥¥¥
Overlooking the Pearl River on sleepy Shamian Island, this opulent hotel is the place to relax in Guangzhou.

For a key to hotel price categories see p148

General Index

Acknowledgments

This edition updated by

Contributor Hillary Leung
Senior Editor Alison McGill
Senior Designer Stuti Tiwari
Project Editors Dipika Dasgupta, Zoë Rutland
Editor Nayan Keshan
Assistant Editors Ilina Choudhary, Anjasi Nongkynrih Nyshadham
Art Editor Bandana Paul
Picture Research Administrator Vagisha Pushp
Publishing Assistant Halima Mohammed
Jacket Designer Jordan Lambley
Senior Cartographer Mohammad Hassan
Cartography Manager Suresh Kumar
DTP Designer Rohit Rojal
Senior Production Editor Jason Little
Senior Production Controller Samantha Cross
Deputy Managing Editor Beverly Smart
Managing Editors Shikha Kulkarni, Hollie Teague
Managing Art Editor Sarah Snelling
Senior Managing Art Editor Priyanka Thakur
Art Director Maxine Pedliham
Publishing Director Georgina Dee

DK would like to thank the following for their contribution to the previous editions: Liam Fitzpatrick, Jason Gagliardi, Andrew Stone, David Leffman, Charles Young, Ruth Reisenberger, Kathryn O'Donoghue, Lee Redmond, Blue Island Publishing, London

The publisher would like to thank the following for their kind permission to reproduce their photographs:
(**Key:** a-above; b-below/bottom; c-centre; f-far; l-left; r-right; t-top)

123RF.com: danielvfung 19tl; Fedor Selivanov 10b.

4Corners: Claudio Cassaro 2tl, 8–9; Günter Gräfenhain 3tl, 62–3; Huw Jones 4cr; Luigi Vaccarella 4crb.

Alamy Images: Asia Photopress 66b; Carlo Bollo 57tl; Andrew Cawley 56b; Pak Hung Chan 59tr; Pavlos Christoforou 58br; Charles Crust 93t; Cultura Creative 14–15c; Foto 28 95bl; FPLA 109cla; Hemis 55tl, 135t; Hemis/Degas Jeanne-Pierre 80tr; Hemis.fr / Jean-Pierre Degas 51t; Bob Henry 4b; imageBROKER/Ingo Schulz 11cla; ImageRite 41tr; Islandspics HK 31bl; JoeFoxBerlin 16bl; JTB Media Creation 84cla; Moon Yin Lam 121cla; Andrew Linscott 108cla; Jon Lord 47tl; Arnel Manalang 32clb; Stefano Politi Markovina 103bl; Hilke Maunder 46t; Kees Metselaar 32br; My Favourite Lens 23bl; Sean Pavone 98–9; Prisma Bildagentur AG/Vidler Steve 83clb, 108b; Radharc Images/Joe Fox 64tl; Radharc Images/Joe Fox 72tr, 97tr; Rosalrene Betancourt 6 11cra; Paul Rushton 45br;

Peter Scholey 47br; SOPA Images Limited 112cra; Dave Stamboulis 29br; Jose Luis Stephens 23tl; Ian Trower 19br; Vinicius Valle 96br; Ron Yue 45cl.

Amaroni's Little Italy: 105br.

Castelo Concepts: 114tl.

Corbis: Bettmann 36b; Massimo Borchi 94tr; Dallas and John Heaton 2tr, 34–5; Destinations 57br; Victor Fraile 136bl; Robert Harding World Imagery/Gavin Hellier 43bl; James Marshall 67bc; Wally McNamee 37br; Redlink/Lo Mak 117br; Ian Trower 131br; 145/Ocean/Wilfred Y Wong 59cl; xPACIFICA 38clb.

Dreamstime.com: Steve Allen 124tl; Tommy Alvén 18crb; Au_yeung225 48tl; Baoshengrulai 89cr; Beibaoke1 7tl; Bjeayes 80cl; Earnesttse 24–5; Evgenia Bolyukh 29tl; Olteanu Calin 123br; Cheechew 120bl; Acon Cheng 125bl; Earnesttse 44t; Efired 4cla; Galinasavina 33clb; Dejia Gao 134cr; Jorg Hackemann 68tl; Hannamariah 137tr; Hkrunning 73tr; Xin Hua 89tl; Hupeng 48c; Jingaiping 94bl, 100cla; Mike K. 61cl, 76tl; Kewuwu 67tl; Kiankhoon 41bl; Sergii Koval 53cla; Kwokfai 86bl; Nohead Lam 16–17; Lance Lee 126tl; Yiu Tung Lee 40bl, 41cla, 106tl; Keng Po Leung 22–3c, 39, 42tc, 81tl; Roland Nagy 10tr; Matee Nuserm 136tr; Ohmaymay 58tl; Leung Cho Pan 6cl, 101tr; Patrickmak039 86t; Paulwongkwan 117tr; Sean Pavone 3tr, 49tl, 65tr, 138–9b; William Perry 21tl; Pindiyath100 11tr, 32–3, 39cr, 48bc, 58c, 76br, 78tr, 82tr, 88br, 89cr, 104bl; Pixattitude 16cl, 101br; Plotnikov 14cla; Poupaep 4t; Saiko3p 39tl, 102t; Sakuragirin 10clb; Stbernardstudio 12cl; StrippedPixel 74t, 87bl, 107br; Kanok Sulaiman 12–3tc; Szefei 52cl; Tktktk 104cra; Torsakarin 52br; Wing Ho Tsang 49cra, 88cla; Thor Jorgen Udvang 6tr; Jeremy Wee 33tl; Ho Nam Wong 111br; Xishuiyuan 132tr; Yourlettertome 125tl; Jess Yu 11crb, 28–9, 31tl, 43cra, 118b, 123tr; Lai Ching Yuen 40tc; Ziggymars 122tl; Zkruger 22clb, 80b.

Fernando's: 129br.

Four Seasons Hotel Hong Kong: 54clb, 71cl.

Getty Images: AFP/Mike Clarke15crb; AFP/Philippe Lopez 68br; Doug Armand 52tl; Virginie Blanquart 131cra; Victor Fraile 61tr; Universal History Archive 36cb; Stefan Irvine 12br; jalvaran 75bl; John Hudson Photography 11bl; Ross Kinnaird 132cb; Loic Lagarde 11br; Paul Lakatos 37cla; Maremagnum 112bl; Thomas Reucker 74bl; rexlam 119cla; Lars Ruecker 53tr; South China Morning Post 55c.

Grand Lisboa: 127bl.

Hong Kong Heritage Museum: 26clb, 26br, 26–7, 27br.

Hongkong Land Limited: www.dadokit.com 69t; Hotel InterContinental, Hong Kong: 90t, 91bl.

iStockphoto.com: ahei 81clb; E+ / Chunyip Wong 107cra; EarnestTse 1; Gfed 20crb; HU-JUN 110t; Sergio Delle Vedove 30–1c; Vicky Lee Kai Wai 79cra; winhorse 68c.

Island Shangri-La: 77cl.

Jin Yong Gallery / Information and Public Relations Section: 27cra.

Mandarin Oriental, Macau: 128t.

Ocean Rock Seafood & Tapas: 20cla.

One Thirty-One: 115br.

Padstow: Lusher Photography / Mary Wong 113cra.

Ritz-Carlton, Hong Kong: 50b.

Robert Harding Picture Library: Amanda Hall 4cl; Fumio Okada 18–19; David Sellwood 118cra; Ian Trower 4clb, 20–21.

Shangri-La International Hotel Management Limited: 133tr.

Shutterstock.com: Hit1912 13clb, lentamart 96tr, Neo Siu 14bc, OSTILL is Franck Camhi 60b.

SuperStock: Juzant 23crb; Iain Masterton 17tr; Steve Vidler 21br.

The Hong Kong Jockey Club: 17bl.

The Landmark Mandarin Oriental: 70t.

The Peninsula Hotel Limited Hong Kong: 41tr, 55b.

The Venetian Macao: Visual Media 127cra.

Cover

Front and spine: **iStockphoto.com:** EartnestTse.

Back: **Alamy Stock Photo:** Asia cla; **Getty Images:** Prisma by Dukas tr, zhuyufang tl; **iStockphoto.com:** EarnestTse.

Pull Out Map Cover

iStockphoto.com: EartnestTse.

All other images © Dorling Kindersley
For further information see: www.dkimages.com

Penguin Random House

First edition in 2002

First published in Great Britain by Dorling Kindersley Limited DK, One Embassy Gardens, 8 Viaduct Gardens, London SW11 7BW, UK

he authorised representative in the EEA is Dorling Kindersley Verlag GmbH. Arnulfstr. 124, 80636 Munich, Germany

Published in the United States by DK Publishing, 1745 Broadway, 20th Floor, New York, NY 10019, USA

Copyright © 2002, 2022 Dorling Kindersley Limited A Penguin Random House Company

22 23 24 25 10 9 8 7 6 5 4 3 2 1

A CIP catalogue record is available from the British Library.

A catalogue record for this book is available from the Library of Congress.

ISSN 1479-344X
ISBN 978-0-2415-6890-3

Printed and bound in Malaysia

www.dk.com

*As a guide to abbreviations in visitor information blocks: **Adm** = admission charge.*